TABLE OF CONTENTS

Page

ACRONYMS

KATUSA	Korean Augmentation to the US Army
KMAG	Korean Military Advisory Group
NKPA	North Korean People's Army
PMAG	Provisional Military Advisory Group
R.O.K.	Republic of Korea
R.O.K.A	Republic of Korea Army
USAFIK	United States Army Forces in Korea
USAMGIK	United States Army Military Government in Korea

TABLES

CHAPTER 1

INTRODUCTION

> You must know something about strategy and tactics and logistics, but also economics and politics and diplomacy and history. You must know everything you can know about military power, and you must also understand the limits of military power.
>
> —President John F. Kennedy,
> Field Manual 3-24, *Counterinsurgency*

The United States of America has been at war with violent extremist organizations since 11 September 2001, aiming to defeat their ability to threaten the security of America.[1] In response, the U.S. Government deployed the U.S. Army to Afghanistan and Iraq. However, America cannot overcome this threat alone because military success in this Global War on Terror requires building host-nation governance and host-nation security force capacity and capability. The U.S. Army and Marine Corps Field Manual (FM) 3-24, *Counterinsurgency*, describes the framework to defeat an insurgency and identifies the development of host-nation security forces as crucial to defeating insurgency networks.[2] Foreign military forces cannot defeat an insurgency without the assistance of local security forces, and can only achieve success by setting conditions by which local security forces provide security for the host-nation populace.[3] Achieving American goals in Iraq and Afghanistan depends upon the competence and capability of local security forces in those nations.[4] At the 2007 Association of the United States Army Conference Secretary Gates stated, ―Arguably, the most important military component in the War on Terror is not the fighting we do ourselves, but how well we enable and empower our partners to defend and govern their own countries.‖[5] Success in the current war does not depend entirely on military force, but force does facilitate

1

necessary security requirements that will allow nonmilitary measures to succeed. Building and partnering with host-nation security forces enables American objectives, and secures American interests abroad against violent extremist organizations and networks.[6]

America currently faces threats from traditional state on state conflicts, transnational actors that threaten American interests across traditional state boundaries, extremist groups, and internationally oriented terrorists.[7] Regardless of where threats may rise, it is essential to understand that the United States lacks sufficient resources and the political will necessary to handle all threats alone. These threats require America to build host-nation security force capacity and capability through security cooperation efforts.[8] The ability to advise foreign forces is central to any security cooperation effort, and studying past conflicts may help the U.S. Army understand how to conduct military advisory operations more effectively.

The Korean Conflict served as the first large scale American effort to build a host-nation security force from the ground up, and the lessons learned are applicable to today's operating environment.[9] This study will look in depth at the tactics, techniques, and procedures used by the U.S. Army Korean Military Advisory Group (KMAG) to train and mentor the Republic of Korea (R.O.K.) Army from 1950 thru 1953, and will shed light on how the KMAG experience can increase the U.S. Army's understanding of what comprises a successful advisory mission. The insights gained from studying KMAG's advisory mission may provide the current force a better appreciation of the intricacies of advising foreign forces in the future.

The U.S. Army defines Security Force Assistance as —unified actin to generate, employ, and sustain local, host nation, or regional security forces in support of a legitimate authority."[10] The U.S. Army has conducted varying levels of Security Force Assistance to train and build host nation forces during multiple conflicts over the last century, beginning with the Philippines, from 1898-1913, to Iraq and Afghanistan today.[11] In each of these conflicts, the U.S. Army has had to create an ad-hoc advisor force because the military failed to sustain interest in training for the advisory mission during peacetime. In between large wars, the U.S Army focused on high intensity combat operations, losing the institutional knowledge and soldier adaptability necessary to conduct military advising of foreign forces. The wars in Afghanistan and Iraq show the U.S. Army re-learning lessons learned from past advisory missions.[12]

The general perception in the U.S. Army is that Special Operations Forces conduct military advisory duty. Special Operations Forces have the required cultural, language, and negotiation training to conduct Security Force Assistance. These soldiers have the training and knowledge to build competent host-nation security forces, but the size and scope of the current mission places the responsibility for training host-nation security forces on conventional personnel.[13] These conventional forces have served as advisors in the Philippines, Korea, Greece, Vietnam, El Salvador, Honduras, Columbia, Afghanistan, and Iraq over the last one-hundred years in an ad-hoc fashion. Regardless, military leadership continues to debate how to prepare the force to conduct effective military advising of host-nation security forces and balance it with preparation for traditional forms of war fighting. Current doctrine attempts to grasp this concept with the development of Full Spectrum Operations, which requires American forces to balance preparation for war with an emphasis on offensive, defensive, and stability operations.[14] Due to the nature of likely future conflicts, conventional forces will be required to conduct military advisory duty of host-nation security forces in the future making it paramount to maintain advisory skills across the force.[15]

Current U.S. Army doctrine places the responsibility of advising and training host-nation security forces on the conventional modular Brigade Combat Team.[16] However, soldiers in these formations lack the required training in competencies necessary to be successful advisors. Leadership in the U.S. Army must prepare conventional forces to be military advisors, seek to understand why advisory techniques worked in the past, and work toward applying them in today's environment. The force must be wary of clinging to techniques for the sake of familiarity, and must foster a constant state of innovative learning.[17] Security Force Assistance education and training must be instilled and interest in advisory fundamentals maintained throughout the conventional force so they may be applied successfully in future operations.

Past conflicts have shown that not all soldiers can advise foreign forces well, and that certain screening processes and procedures can ensure selection of the most capable advisors. Soldiers need more advanced language proficiency combined with cultural understanding so that they can immerse themselves in local populations. Culture develops in societies through language, and language is the mechanism that transmits culture from one generation to another.[18] In this regard, language training and cultural training form a symbiotic relationship that helps prepare soldiers to understand their environment while working with host-nation security forces.

Most soldiers will not become experts in host-nation languages, but should have at least a rudimentary knowledge of local languages. Advisors who do not attempt to learn the local language will not be able to immerse themselves effectively in the culture of the nation they are supporting, or be able to connect with host-nation counterparts at anything beyond a superficial level, potentially leading to a misunderstanding of the nation around them.[19] Counterinsurgency expert David Kilcullen states, ―The capabilities required are akin to author Rudyard Kipling's Colonel Creighton in the novel *Kim*–a deep knowledge of language, ethnography, geography, and history.‖[20] Robert Ramsey of the Combat Studies Institute points out the following criteria for creating a capable advisory force. Advisors must undergo in depth training covering the culture, language, procedures, capabilities, and limitations of the host-nation prior to conducting advisor duties. Longer and repetitive advisory tours may be necessary to build rapport with host nation counterparts and advisor proficiency. Ultimately, advisory success depends upon the support structure established between the advisor, host nation, and the U.S. chain of command.[21] Developing language and cultural competency in the conventional force are crucial steps towards success in advising host-nation counterparts. Ignorance of culture and language will deny soldiers the ability to build relationships with the local people, and ultimately lead to the failure of American objectives.[22]

Drawing lessons from the Korean military advisory mission will enhance future Security Force Assistance efforts. Sixty years of scholarship are available to help understand KMAG efforts to advise and assist the R.O.K. Army during the Korean War. Most of this literature examines events after the invasion of South Korea by North Korea on 25 June 1950. Few scholars have studied the post-World War II period, and the

American effort to bolster the R.O.K. Government. The U.S. Government developed advisor initiatives for South Korean Air Force, Coast Guard, and police forces but this thesis examines only KMAG advisory actions with the Republic of Korea Army from 1950 to 1953. Access to North Korean archives limits this research to Western interpretations of the Korean conflict. Moreover, few sources deal extensively with the Korean Military Advisory Group.

To understand KMAG it is necessary to examine the politico-military environment following the allied occupation of Korea in 1945.[23] United States Army advisory initiatives in South Korea slowly developed from 1945 to 1949 with the establishment of KMAG on 28 April 1949. American commitment to the R.O.K. Army expanded after the North Korean invasion on 25 June 1950. An analysis of KMAG doctrine, organization, and training will facilitate an understanding of the transformation of the R.O.K. Army from 1950 to 1953. This study will compare the R.O.K. Army that existed after its devastating defeat by the North Korean Army in 1950 with the R.O.K. Army of 1953 in order to understand how the U.S. Army helped develop the South Korean Army. Additionally, this study will compare the Korean advisory mission to the current advisory mission in Iraq, with the goal of gaining insights for future Security Force Assistance endeavors. The current advisory mission in Iraq is mature and provides the opportunity for direct comparison of current advisory actions with those of the Korean Conflict.

---

[1]—President Bush addresses the Nation," *Washington Post,* 20 September 2001, http://www.washingtonpost.com/wpsrv/nation/specials/attacked/transcripts/bushaddress _092001.html (accessed 21 November 2010). Congress did not officially declare war against terrorism after the terrorist attacks of 11 September 2001. The President, George

W. Bush, announced a war on terrorism in a speech before a joint session of Congress on 20 September 2001. In the speech President Bush announced that —Our war on terror begins with Al-Qaeda (the terrorist network associated with bin Laden), but it does not end there. It will not end until every terrorist group of global reach has been found, stopped, and defeated."

[2]U.S. Army, Field Manual 3-24, *Counterinsurgency* (Washington, DC: Government Printing Office, 2006), 6-1.

[3]John Nagl, *Learning to Eat Soup with a Knife* (Chicago: University of Chicago Press, 2005), xiv.

[4]John Nagl, —Institutionalizing Adaptation: It's Time for a Permanent Advisor Command," *Military Review* (September-October 2008): 21.

[5]Joint Center for Security Force Assistance. *Security Force Assistance Planner's Guide* (Washington, DC: Government Printing Office, December 2009), 1.

[6]David J. Kilcullen, *Counterinsurgency* (New York: Oxford University Press, 2010), 220.

[7]David J. Kilcullen, *The Accidental Guerilla: Fighting Small Wars in the Midst of a Big One* (New York: Oxford University Press, 2009), 40.

[8]Ibid., 41.

[9]Sheila Jager, —Iraqi Security Forces and Lessons from Korea," *Strategic Studies Institute Editorial* (December 2006), 211.

[10]U.S. Army, Field Manual 3-07.1, *Security Force Assistance* (Washington, DC: Government Printing Office, 2009), 1-1.

[11]Andrew J. Birtle, —Pacing the Philippines," in *U.S. Army Counterinsurgency and Contingency Operations Doctrine 1860-1941* (Washington, DC: Center of Military History, 2003), 153.

[12]John Nagl, *Institutionalizing Adaptation: It's time for a Permanent Army Advisor Corps* (Washington, DC: Center for a New American Security, June 2007), 4.

[13]U.S. Army, Field Manual 3-24, *Counterinsurgency*, 6-3.

[14]U.S. Army, Field Manual 7-0, *Training for Full Spectrum Operations* (Washington, DC: Government Printing Office, 2008), 1-7.

[15]Robert Ramsey, *Advising Indigenous Forces: American Advisors in Korea, Vietnam, and El Salvador* (Fort Leavenworth, KS: Combat Studies Institute Press, 2006), 2.

[16]U.S. Army, Field Manual 3-07.1, *Security Force Assistance*, iv. U.S. Army Field Manual 3-07.1 states that the Combined Arms Doctrine Directorate, Combined Arms Center is responsible for sustaining interest in the advisory mission and maintaining Security Force Assistance. The Combined Arms Doctrine Directorate places Security Force Assistance responsibility on conventional U.S. Army forces.

[17]Kilcullen, *Counterinsurgency*, 222.

[18]Jeff Watson, —Language and Culture Training: Separate Paths," *Military Review* (March-April 2010): 95.

[19]William Lederer and Eugene Burdick, *The Ugly American* (New York: W. W. Norton and Company, Inc., 1986), 276.

[20]Kilcullen, *Counterinsurgency*, 223. Rudyard Kipling's novel *Kim* takes place in British ruled India. COL Creighton is a British officer in the story who displays remarkable cultural competence in India.

[21]Selected Papers of the 2007 Conference of Army Historians. *The U.S. Army and Irregular Warfare 1775-2007*, ed. Richard G. Davis (Washington, DC: Center of Military History, 2008), 11.

[22]Greg Mortenson and David Relin, *Three Cups of Tea* (New York: Penguin Group, 2006), 310.

[23]Roy Appleman, *U.S. Army in the Korean War: South to the Naktong, North to the Yalu* (Washington, DC: Center of Military History, 1961), 4. U.S. forces accepted the surrender of the Japanese south of the 38th parallel in Korea on 9 September 1945. The U.S. Army controlled the newly formed South Korea under the banner of the U.S. Army Military Government in Korea until 15 August 1948, when South Koreans formed the government of the Republic of Korea.

CHAPTER 2

THE DEVELOPMENT OF KMAG

During World War II, the Allied Powers of the United States, Great Britain, and the Soviet Union cooperated to defeat Germany and Japan. In December 1943, with the outcome of the war still uncertain, the United States made an open-ended political and military commitment to a free and independent Korea in the Cairo Declaration.[1] After the defeat of Germany in May 1945, the Soviet Union pledged to attack the Japanese on the continent of Asia, thus beginning political maneuvers for control of Korea. As the end of the war in the Pacific loomed, the United States attempted to deny Soviet influence in the region by forcing a Japanese surrender prior to Soviet intervention against Japan. Soviet military forces moved quickly, ultimately forcing American diplomats to negotiate for Soviet occupation of Korea north of the 38th parallel.[2] The U.S. struck a diplomatic agreement with the Soviet Union that limited the Soviet advance to the 38th parallel. Meanwhile, American forces prepared for a large assault on Japan, but use of the atomic bomb ended the war without invasion of the Japanese mainland.[3]

On 10 August 1945, the U.S. State War-Navy Coordinating Committee decided to intervene in Korea after the fall of Japan for fear of the Soviet Army overrunning all of Manchuria and the Korean peninsula.[4] Contrary to the State War-Navy Coordinating Committee, General Douglas MacArthur, commander of all Allied Pacific Forces, viewed the occupation of Japan as a priority for his forces and essential in denying Soviet influence over East Asia.[5] MacArthur considered the American occupation of Korea unnecessary, but the administration ordered him to commit forces to Korea because the Soviets rapidly swept across the Yalu River and occupied the Korean peninsula north of the 38th parallel. It took American military planners sixteen days to counter the Soviet advance by altering the invasion plan for Japan to include movement of three divisions from Okinawa and the Philippines to Korea.[6] The U.S. Army occupied Korea south of the 38th parallel in order to disarm the Japanese military, maintain a U.S. presence on the peninsula to prevent the complete Soviet occupation of Korea, and establish rule of law. However, Korea was not the priority for the United States; General Douglas MacArthur, head of the Pacific Campaign, and U.S. President Harry Truman focused a majority of their effort on occupying Japan at the end of World War II to prevent Soviet interference in Japan. General MacArthur continued to ignore Korea in the coming years because he saw Japan as the strategic priority.[7]

In July 1945, the Allied leaders of World War II attended the Potsdam Conference to discuss the status of the post war world. During the meeting, the United States maneuvered to deny communist expansion.[8] Immediately, the United States and the Soviet Union began competing for influence over the political fate of Korea. America entered Korea in September of 1945, without a clear understanding of the political objectives defined in President Harry S. Truman's new policy of communist containment.[9] Prior to the fall of Japan, the Pentagon showed no long-term interest in Korea, but the new policy of communist containment required the U.S. military to commit resources to Korea.[10] Following the Moscow Conference on 27 December 1945, the United States and the Soviet Union agreed to administer the country under a U.S.-Soviet Joint Commission, with an agreed goal of an independent Korea after five years of international oversight.[11] The Soviet Union grudgingly agreed to the terms of the Moscow Conference knowing that it would stall the creation of a communist state north of the 38th Parallel in Korea.[12] At the time, South Korea did not factor in to Stalin's

Soviet-bloc expansion plan, but the U.S. administration remained convinced that the

Soviet Union threatened U.S. interests.[13] However, both the U.S. and the Soviet Union

approved Korean-led governments in their respective areas of occupation, each of which

was favorable to the occupying power's political ideology. The United States chose to

limit South Korea's ability to conduct armed aggression for fear of sparking war with the

Soviet Union. Meanwhile, the Soviet Union supplied North Korea with a large arsenal of

formidable weapons.[14]

Following liberation, Korea experienced internal upheavals in each occupied

zone.[15] The United States denied communist movements south of the 38th parallel to

ensure the establishment of democratic rule. Meanwhile, the Soviet controlled North

denied democratic movements in order to establish communist rule. Additionally,

incompetence burdened U.S. civil administration efforts in Korea. The United States

Army Forces in Korea (USAFIK) organized around the U.S. XXIV Corps, led by

Lieutenant General John Hodge, initially attempted to establish civil control by

reinstating the police force that had served during Japanese rule. Hodge realized the

Korean people hated the police force because it was rife with brutality and corruption, but

he had no alternative to establish civil control. In Hodge's opinion, American troops

lacked the training and experience needed for law enforcement.[16] Hodge received

directives from Washington to establish a government in "harmony with U.S. policies

toward Korea," when in fact no policies existed and the State Department knew little

about the country except that Koreans wanted unity and independence.[17] To quell the

power of rising political parties Hodge created The United States Army Military

Government in Korea (USAMGIK) to show that only one government was in charge of South Korea.[18] Establishing USAMGIK made many Koreans feel that Americans simply replaced the Japanese as the new colonial ruler.[19] Amplifying this feeling, USAMGIK imposed strict curfews on the citizens of Seoul adding to the unrest in the population.[20] Additionally, USAMGIK created an economic crisis by attempting to reform rice production, thus driving down the price of South Korea's main economic staple.[21] These measures confused the South Korean population and helped foster a pro-communist insurgency in South Korea.[22] To be fair, the U.S. Army XXIV Corps that formed USAMGIK lacked the political, social, and economic experience needed to establish civil control.[23] Many of the soldiers comprising XXIV Corps were veterans of the Pacific in World War II and unhappy about not returning home; this sentiment negatively affected their performance of occupation duties.[24]

In an effort to remedy the mistakes made in American occupation efforts, Lieutenant General Hodge disbanded all remaining Japanese-built governmental institutions and started creating new Korean-led ones. Despite Hodge's institutional reorganization, many former Japanese era Korean officials remained in charge of Korean institutions due to their qualifications and education, casting a dark shadow on U.S.-Korean relations.[25] As dissatisfaction with the U.S. occupation increased, Hodge began looking for local Korean solutions to peacekeeping and law enforcement problems. Consequently, he abolished the Japanese police force because of its repressive measures and replaced it with the Korean National Civil Police Agency.[26] USAMGIK re-established the Korean Police Academy in Seoul in October of 1945 to begin training new South Korean police forces with a one-month basic training regimen.[27] Interestingly,

British officer T. E. Lawrence came to the same conclusion dealing with Arabs during World War I. Concluding during his time as an advisor in Arabia that "it is better to let the locals do it tolerably than you do it perfectly." Indigenous solutions are preferable as the local population more easily accepts them.[28]

In addition, the leadership at USAMGIK recognized that the U.S. sponsored government of Korea needed to establish its own organization to handle internal security and defend its borders.[29] Lieutenant General Hodge was interested in establishing a South Korean Army at the onset of American occupation, but the U.S. blocked this effort for fear of upsetting the Soviet Union.[30] Hodge continued to push for a South Korean national defense force and on 13 November 1945, he established the Office of National Defense to develop future national defense efforts. Initial assessments by USAMGIK staff recommended a 25,000-man police force and a 45,000-man Korean National Defense Force comprising an army corps, of three infantry divisions and an air force. USAMGIK stressed quality over quantity, requiring volunteers to fill the national defense force.[31] This measure was Korea's first step towards establishing a permanent national defense force but it must be emphasized that USAMGIK could not implement it without permission from a U.S. administration that feared sparking a confrontation with the Soviet Union. The Soviet-controlled north and the U.S.-controlled south were cautious of military buildup on either side. Thus, U.S. policy makers in Washington D.C. delayed the establishment of a Korean defense force. Instead, the United States transferred U.S. arms and equipment to the Korean National Civil Police to relieve the U.S. Army of civil police duties.[32] Additionally, USAMGIK tried to take advantage of leftover Japanese arms and equipment in an effort to arm the proposed Korean defense force, but, unfortunately General MacArthur's Headquarters in Japan issued a directive for the destruction of all Japanese equipment. Nevertheless, 60,000 rifles and 15 rounds of ammunition per rifle were set aside in warehouses for the future Korean Army.[33]

The Moscow Conference of 1945, which established a joint U.S.-Soviet trusteeship of the two Koreas, dissolved during multiple meetings held between 1945 and 1947. The Soviet Union and the United States intentionally failed to reach an agreement over how to unify Korea to protect their respective national interests, further dividing the country and reducing hopes of unification.[34] Following the collapse of the Moscow Agreement, American efforts focused on the establishment of an anti-communist Republic of Korea in the south, led by the nationalist Dr. Rhee Syngman.[35] In the north, the Soviet Union established the Communist Democratic People's Republic of Korea under the leadership of Kim il Sung and promptly worked to arm and defend it.[36] Both Syngman and Kim garnered massive public support from Korean nationals because of their steadfast opposition to Japanese rule.[37] The division between the two Koreas caused the inevitable military confrontation between the nationalist south and communist north.[38]

The dissolving Moscow Agreement and potential future confrontation with the Soviet backed north spurred USAMGIK to renew efforts to create a South Korean National Defense Force. In addition to protecting South Korea, Lieutenant General Hodge believed the new defense force might become a force that represented the South Korean populace and serve as a viable alternative to the Japanese influenced Korean National Police.[39] By 1946, USAMGIK efforts to create a National Defense Force took the form of an aggressive recruiting program, aimed at finding the best officer candidates in South Korea. In addition, USAMGIK nationalized many of the private militias that sprang up after the Japanese lost control to form the nucleus of the fledgling South Korean National Defense Force.[40]

Significantly, USAMGIK planners recognized the need for a U.S. advisory mission to help build the Korean national defense force.[41] Few Koreans could speak English, creating an obstacle to any U.S. advisory mission. In order to remedy this, USAMGIK established a language school to teach Korean officers basic English. Interestingly, no military planners acknowledged the need for American advisors to learn Korean.[42] This language-training program introduced South Korean officers to English language and culture. It established a common foundation between South Korean officers and future U.S. military advisors, providing South Koreans insight on how to work with American counterparts. Interestingly, USAMGIK did not develop a program to train U.S. military advisors how to work with South Korean counterparts.

The Office of National Defense and the Bureau of National Police worked together to provide internal security to South Korea. By the end of March 1946, USAMGIK altered the national defense apparatus by removing the Bureau of National Police from the Office of National Defense. This split allowed the Korean National Police to focus on law enforcement and internal security while the charter of the National Defense office was to defend the sovereign rights of South Korea. Additionally, USAMGIK altered the whole of government by creating departments for all Korean governmental elements. In keeping with Soviet sensitivity, USAMGIK renamed the Office of National Defense the Department of Internal Security on 15 June 1946.[43] The fledgling Department of Internal Security remained a secondary effort for USAMGIK, with the bulk of funding and resources allocated to the Korean National Police. Ultimately, this affected early American advisory missions because of under- funding and a lack of quality equipment with which to outfit the defense force.[44]

Lieutenant General Hodge assigned Colonel Arthur Champeny, the first Director of National Defense, to create a plan for a Korean national defense force. Champeny developed a plan called BAMBOO, proposing a 25,000-man constabulary police reserve armed with light infantry weapons and basic infantry training. Hodge approved Champeny's plan, and the Constabulary formed in January 1946.[45] Plan BAMBOO called for the establishment of U.S.-style infantry company-sized elements, without heavy weapons platoons, with one unit assigned to each of the country's eight provinces. USAMGIK assigned six U.S. advisors, (two officers, and four enlisted soldiers), to advise each company. The Constabulary companies expanded into eight provincial regiments by having the South Koreans conduct their own recruiting and training.[46] As a result of the limited advisory mission, recruit training relied on South Koreans experienced with Japanese tactics to train a Constabulary styled in the image of the U.S. Army.[47] This training proved ineffective and counterproductive, thus showing the need for a larger advisory mission to the Constabulary.

USAMGIK established the Korean Training Center in Seoul to build an officer corps to lead the Constabulary. The Korean Training Center commissioned officers in conjunction with an English language school.[48] Ideal candidates lacked ties to the Japanese occupation, but inevitably, qualified officer candidates came with colonial Japanese experience. USAMGIK recognized the importance of using experienced Japanese officers because these men would lead much of the basic training for

16

Constabulary soldiers.[49] However, all Korean officer candidates were untrained in modern U.S. Army tactics, and insisted on using Japanese banzai tactics with their hallmarks of poor marksmanship. This Japanese influence hindered advisory efforts to style the Constabulary after the U.S. Army.[50] The first 110 officers of the future South Korean army received their commission within four months of the establishment of the Constabulary. Only two of the officers had not served in the colonial Japanese Army. Future Korean Training Center classes continued to graduate Constabulary officers with Japanese experience, impeding the advisory mission to build an army in an image of the United States.[51]

The American advisory mission was essential to the formation of the Constabulary. Remarkably, a junior officer had an important impact on the future army of South Korea. In July 1946, Captain James H. Hausman was assigned to USAMGIK as an advisor to the Eighth Constabulary Regiment at Ch'unch'on in Kangwon province, forty-five miles northeast of Seoul. His previous U.S. Army experience involved a distinguished yearlong combat tour in Europe during World War II. Prior to World War II, he trained Women's Army Corps enlistees in Iowa and Florida. Ten years of experience in peace and war prepared him for unique challenges in Korea.[52] Captain Hausman displayed an uncanny rapport with Korean counterparts that permitted him to establish the Constabulary training initiatives that formed the foundation of future Republic of Korea Army training.

Lieutenant Colonel Russell D. Barros headed the small and sparsely resourced advisory group that Hausman joined in 1946. Barros had Hausman transferred to the Bureau of Constabulary in Seoul and told him to focus on expanding the advisory mission.[53] Peter Clemens writes that Hausman, —dominated the small advisory group, was given carte blanche to implement his ideas, and left indelible changes on what became the South Korean Army."[54] Hausman arguably had the greatest effect on the Constabulary of any officer serving in Korea between 1946 and 1948.[55]

USAMGIK efforts to expand the Constabulary to its authorized strength of 25,000 personnel failed due to growing political unrest in South Korea and a lack of American resources. Contrarily, USAMGIK invested 60 percent of the South Korean security budget in the National Police still seeing them as more effective than the Constabulary.[56] The lack of funding and resources kept provincial regiments at battalion strength or below, and limited the Constabulary's ability to train and operate as an army.[57] Hausman attempted to improve efficiency in the organization by informing the Director of the Department of Internal Security, Brigadier General William L. Roberts, to relinquish control of the Constabulary to the Constabulary advisory group. Hausman argued that two headquarters should not be attempting to run the same organization, and Roberts acted quickly by separating the two. From that point forward, the Department of Internal Security handled policy, and the advisory group of the Constabulary acted as the military headquarters responsible for Constabulary operations.[58] Additionally, Roberts actively pursued assigning personnel with combat experience to advisory duty in order to give the best possible training to the fledgling Korean defense force.[59]

During this same time, South Korea was taking steps toward self-rule. On 20 July 1948, elections held south of the 38th parallel chose a National Assembly to draft a constitution. Members of the National Assembly elected Dr. Rhee Syngman as the first President of South Korea. On 15 August 1948, Rhee announced the formation of the

18

Republic of Korea (R.O.K.) south of the 38th parallel. The formation of the R.O.K. dissolved U.S. Army control of the government of South Korea through USAMGIK. A self-ruling South Korea allowed USAFIK to begin a phased withdrawal and hand over security responsibilities to Korean security forces. At this time, Major General John B. Coulter replaced Lieutenant General Hodge as commander of USAFIK. Prior to Hodge leaving South Korea, President Rhee struck an agreement with Hodge to have U.S. forces turnover weapons and equipment to South Korea as soldiers re-deployed to the United States. Additionally, U.S. President Harry Truman appointed Ambassador John Muccio as Special Representative to Korea in charge of the American Mission in Korea. Muccio's main task was negotiating withdrawal of U.S. troops, except for a small contingent of advisors for the newly formed Constabulary.[60]

An autonomous Korea had major effects on the Constabulary force. USAFIK reorganized the advisory group under the title Provisional Military Advisory Group (PMAG) on 24 August 1948, with Brigadier General Roberts commanding the new organization. PMAG continued to equip and train the fledgling Constabulary force with 241 assigned advisors, a monumental increase in personnel over previous efforts. Prior to the establishment of PMAG, the advisory mission numbered less than one hundred personnel. This increase in advisors still could not cover the expanding Korean forces.[61] Nevertheless, Roberts immediately affected the organization, increased PMAG advisors to 248, flattened bureaucracy, and increased training opportunities for the Constabulary.[52] Interestingly, the Korean government began referring to the Constabulary as the National Defense Army but Americans still refused to recognize it as an army for fear of upsetting the Soviet Union.[63]

The haste of the American withdrawal from South Korea posed problems for its security. In September 1948, as American forces prepared to leave the R.O.K., the Koreans north of the 38th parallel formed the Democratic People's Republic of Korea with the backing of the Soviet Union. The United Nations General Assembly, still seeking a unified Korea looked on as the Soviet Union pledged to leave the Democratic People's Republic of Korea within a year. By November 1948, the U.S. State Department recognized that Soviet motives for leaving Korea, and pressure by the international community for U.S. withdrawal left South Korean security vulnerable to North Korean aggression. The U.S. slowed the removal of troops from South Korea to stabilize the situation. Additionally, South Korean President Rhee Syngman sent a plea to President Truman to slow the U.S. withdrawal until the Republic of Korea security forces could handle internal and external security threats.[64] This action temporarily halted U.S. troop re-deployment, but by December 1948 Far East Command resumed troop withdrawal and scaled back USAFIK forces to one regimental combat team in accordance with the U.N mandate passed on 12 December 1948.[65]

The upstart Constabulary continued to grow through 1948 receiving weapons and equipment from re-deploying U.S. troops. The Constabulary grew by an additional six regiments, but had to its growth because its expansion outpaced equipment turnover by the Americans.[66] As the Constabulary continued to grow, they faced their first major challenge in October of 1948. Small rebellions were common in South Korea, but communist infiltration of the security apparatus boiled into a full revolt. Communist guerrillas rioted on the tiny island of Cheju-Do requiring the South Korean Government to declare martial law and prepare Constabulary troops for movement to the island.[67] On

20

19 October 1948, the 14th Regiment of the Constabulary stationed at Yosu activated for deployment to Cheju-Do, but mutinied. North Korean communist supporters inside the regiment sparked the mutiny, and captured the town of Yosu because they wanted to establish communist rule in South Korea.[68] Over the next few days, the revolt spread to the surrounding villages of Kwangyang, Posong, and Kurye. Significantly, the revolt occurred while President Rhee was visiting General MacArthur in Tokyo.[69] No U.S. troops were available to stomp out the crisis due to the end of the U.S. occupation, requiring the Constabulary to squash the rebellion. Immediately, PMAG advisors and loyal Constabulary regiments organized in an ad-hoc fashion to quell the uprising outside the coastal town of Yosu. PMAG worked diligently with Constabulary senior leadership to prevent disaster, but initial attempts to halt the rebellion required USAFIK to order that advisors take charge of the operation to bring the incident under control.[70] Major General Roberts, the PMAG Commander, advised the Constabulary to crush the revolt with overwhelming force.[71]

The communist insurgents held the town of Yosu for a week but by the end of October, the Constabulary and the Korean National Police suppressed the rebellion. PMAG advisors played a crucial role in the success of the Constabulary from the strategic to the tactical level.[72] Throughout the operation, advisors worked closely with their counterparts to provide combat multipliers such as intelligence, reconnaissance aircraft, and transport aircraft.[73] The operation was not flawless but proved that the Constabulary could handle security at home with support from PMAG advisors.[74] Significantly, the Yosu Rebellion served as the first major operation conducted by the Constabulary and allowed employment of units on a major scale.[75] Consequently, the

Yosu Rebellion highlighted many problems ailing the fledgling Constabulary force that advisors needed to fix if the Constabulary was to become an effective army. These problems included severe fratricide, because of a lack of fire discipline with small arms and machine guns, an inability to coordinate for timely and accurate indirect fires, and a lack of education in small unit tactics. Even with the problems, PMAG advisors proved to themselves that the counterpart relationship worked, even with language and cultural barriers, and developed measurable rapport with Constabulary officers for their actions in the Yosu Rebellion.[76] This experience prepared the advisors to create a R.O.K. Army and it outlined the major problems advisors faced in the years to come.

The Yosu Rebellion made many Koreans question President Rhee's ability to secure South Korea, and required the new government to make major changes to the Constabulary force. The R.O.K. government purged over 1,500 communists from the Constabulary force to deny further uprisings across South Korea.[77] Additionally, the R.O.K. Government screened future members of the Constabulary for political reliability.[78] The final evolution of the Constabulary occurred on 15 December 1948 when it re-flagged to become the R.O.K. Army.[79] All Constabulary schools, training centers and units established by PMAG transitioned to the R.O.K. Army.[80] All six Constabulary Brigades transitioned to R.O.K. Army Divisions and the Koreans pursued an aggressive recruiting and equipping campaign. General Macarthur approved an expansion of the R.O.K. Army to 50,000 Soldiers in February of 1948, but the new South Korean government kept up recruiting pressure and by March 1949, the R.O.K. Army comprised over 65,000 soldiers.[81]

On 2 April 1949, USAFIK received its order to re-deploy all U.S. Forces except for PMAG. Before USAFIK departed, it expanded PMAG so it could advise South Korean units down to the battalion level.[82] Previous U.S. advisor experience in Greece showed the necessity for supervising training at the battalion level to instruct and correct tactical proficiency.[83] On 28 April 1949, Ambassador Muccio sent a message to U.S. Secretary of State George C. Marshall that announced the establishment of the Korean Military Advisory Group (KMAG). Muccio praised the efforts of PMAG and its Korean counterparts, and was impressed that the advisor group had –contributed significantly to raising the capabilities of the security forces of the Republic of Korea."[84] On 1 July 1949, the U.S. Government officially recognized the formation of KMAG, and Brigadier General William L. Roberts assumed duties as the first KMAG commander. The KMAG organization grew to 500 advisory personnel, doubling the size of the PMAG advisory mission.[85] Due to the redeployment of USAFIK, responsibility for soldiers assigned to KMAG fell directly under the American Mission in Korea led by Ambassador Muccio.[86] Immediately, Roberts created standards for the new advisory group focusing on the development of R.O.K. internal security, and building an army capable of defending South Korea. He published an advisors handbook that laid out standards for training the R.O.K. Army and distributed it to all members of KMAG. Additionally, KMAG conducted orientation meetings for new advisors to ensure that new soldiers understood the intent of the advisory mission.[87]

Even with the U.S. withdrawal of combat troops and the end of occupation duties, American economic involvement in South Korea continued to grow. Politicians in Washington D.C. understood that the Japanese and South Korean economies were intermingled, serving American interests as a foothold against communist expansion, but fiscal responsibility marked politics in the U.S. through 1950-1951. The American administration looked to cut special projects across the world from the budget, including South Korea. Even though American economic and military policies in Korea aided communist containment, the U.S. administration pushed towards leaving Korea.[88] Muccio's cable to the Secretary of State establishing KMAG highlights the American desire to leave Korea to its own destiny.[89] American politics negatively influenced KMAG's ability to improve the R.O.K. Army and prepare it for war. U.S. political pressure forced General Roberts to begin planning for the curtailment of the military advisory mission in Korea despite the fact that the R.O.K. Army was not ready to defend South Korea."[90]

Concurrent to the creation of the R.O.K. Army, North Korea established the North Korean People's Army (NKPA) on 8 February 1948. As the KMAG mission suffered from American fiscal responsibility, the NKPA was growing steadily. Soviet advisors assisted with the recruiting, equipping, and training of two full strength infantry divisions and one full strength armor battalion, equipped with Soviet-made T-34 tanks. This concerned South Korea because the R.O.K. Army had no heavy equipment such as artillery and tanks.

Russian and Chinese officials held a meeting in early 1950 to explore the feasibility of attacking South Korea with the North Korean Army. They decided to equip the NKPA with the necessary equipment to invade South Korea. By June 1950, the NKPA comprised seven full strength motorized divisions and an armored brigade. Korean veterans of the Chinese Communist forces made up one third of the NKPA, providing combat tested and trained leaders for the rapidly expanding army. Prior to invading South Korea the NKPA established three additional divisions, and two additional independent regiments. The NKPA had 135,000 personnel fully equipped and trained for combat.[91] In contrast, R.O.K. Army strength numbered close to 100,000 men when combined with the National Police, but their equipment and training did not equal that of the NKPA. In early 1950, the R.O.K. Army finally received U.S. equipment to establish a battalion of artillery and anti-tank companies within half of their infantry regiments. The R.O.K. Army had no armor units, and still lacked air defense assets, and a logistics infrastructure.[92]

President Rhee Syngman saw conflict with North Korea as inevitable and provoked action from the Democratic People's Republic of Korea by conducting border skirmishes throughout 1949 using the R.O.K. Army and National Police.[93] KMAG advisors continued to train the R.O.K. Army throughout this uncertain period, and continued to report the lack of progress in the units they were advising caused by U.S. funding restraints.[94] However, the KMAG Commander, Brigadier General William L. Roberts, relayed a different message to his subordinates and the U.S. Administration.[95] His message painted a falsely optimistic picture. He declared to the administration that, —If South Korea were attacked today by the inferior ground forces of North Korea, plus their Air Corps, I feel that South Korea would take a bloody nose."[96] Meanwhile, the American Mission in Korea painted an even rosier picture with a report that asserted the R.O.K. Army could defeat any invasion from North Korea. Lastly, on 20 June 1949, during a visit of senior military leadership to Korea, Roberts told the Chairman of the Joint Chiefs of Staff, General Omar Bradley, and Army Chief of Staff, General J. Lawton

Collins, that the R.O.K. Army was —the best doggone shooting army outside of the United States." The American administration now believed that the R.O.K. ARMY could repel a North Korean invasion.[97]

On 25 June 1950, the NKPA invaded South Korea with an early morning artillery and mortar barrage. Ten Divisions worth of combat power supported by tanks and ample artillery led a four-prong assault across the 38th parallel slowed more by terrain than the defense of the R.O.K. Army. The ferocity of the assault sent the R.O.K. Army reeling southward abandoning equipment and losing any semblance of order amidst the chaos.[98] The R.O.K. Army began the fight with 98,000 men but could only account for 22,000 men by the end of the first month of fighting.[99] The R.O.K.A. lost 77 percent of its combat power in a matter of days due to poor intelligence of the enemy advance, weak defensive positions, and ambitious war-plans that did not match the capability of the army at the onset of invasion.[100] Units did not maximize terrain advantages to channelize and contain the enemy assault. Obviously, Brigadier General Roberts rosy assessment of the R.O.K. Army was wrong because KMAG failed to equip and train a R.O.K. Army capable of defending South Korea. Fortunately, KMAG advisors stepped in, took de-facto command of R.O.K. Army units, and established hasty R.O.K.A. defensive positions. They organized retreating units and prevented the complete collapse of South Korea.[101]

When the DPRK invaded the Republic of Korea, President Truman committed the United States to the defense of South Korea, surprising the Soviet backed North Korea. American backing of South Korean forces caught the Soviet Union off-guard because it missed the United Nations Security Council meeting discussing Korea, during which the

U.S. promised to support South Korea in the conflict.[102] The Soviet delegate, Yakov

Malik, walked out of the Security Council in protest earlier in the year over the United

Nation's refusal to recognize Communist China instead of the U.S. backed Nationalists.

Malik did not attend the 25 June 1950 meeting, thus allowing a 9-0 vote in favor of

calling for the withdrawal of North Korean forces south of the 38th parallel. Historically

the vote is an anomaly because of the 100 percent voting requirement necessary for the

Security Council to support one combatant against another.[103] The Security Council

Resolution allowed U.S. forces to support the conflict in North Korea under the United

Nations flag lessening the likelihood of direct confrontation with the Soviet Union.[104] By

27 June 1950, President Truman authorized U.S. air and sea forces to support the South

Korean government and began working with Far East Command to send ground units to

aid the R.O.K. Army in defense of South Korea.[105]

As the United Nations convened, the heavily armed, well trained, and offensively

oriented North Korean Army devastated the South Korean Army. No U.S. troops were

available to reinforce the South Korean Army due to the withdrawal of U.S. combat

troops over the previous five years. Ambassador Muccio notified Far East Command,

commanded by General Douglas MacArthur, about the invasion. MacArthur responded

by launching air and naval attacks against the North Korean military.[106] Immediate U.S.

ground support was unavailable because it would have to deploy from Japan or the

Philippines. On 30 June 1950, President Truman escalated American commitment to

Korea by ordering immediate U.S. ground forces to aid the R.O.K. Army.[107] United

States ground forces took time to deploy, and the delay in their arrival in South Korea

allowed the North Korean Army to seize the South's capitol city, Seoul.[108]

U.S. war-plans required all American personnel to evacuate South Korea during an invasion by North Korea. However, many KMAG advisors ignored the guidance and remained with their counterparts. These advisors found themselves organizing the retreat of the South Korean Army while in contact with the enemy.[109] KMAG advisors became the only link between the R.O.K. Army and the Far East Command. General MacArthur attempted to calm the situation by assuring R.O.K. Army commanders U.S. support through his radio messages. KMAG radio operators working out of mobile command posts received the messages and relayed them to R.O.K. Army commanders. These messages persuaded R.O.K. Army leaders to stop retreating, reform, and hold the line for an American counterattack.[110]

By the end of June 1950, the North Koreans controlled all territory north of the Han River, and had killed or captured over half the R.O.K.A. On 1 July 1950, the first U.S. troops arrived to reinforce the R.O.K. Army. The Eighth U.S. Army assumed responsibility for all combat forces in Korea including KMAG. Advisors assigned to the R.O.K. Army continued to fall under KMAG Headquarters for administrative purposes, but were operationally controlled by Eighth U.S. Army Headquarters. Not surprisingly, advisors received conflicting guidance from both organizations over how and where to employ the R.O.K.A.[111] Additionally, the R.O.K. Army command structure was in shambles requiring advisors to lead R.O.K. Army units until they could be re-established.[112] On 9 August 1950, KMAG received authorization from Far East Command to begin increasing the R.O.K. Army end strength.[113]

On 15 September 1950, the Americans launched a daring amphibious assault at Inchon, routing the NKPA and forcing them back across the 38th parallel. The American goal was to unify the Korean peninsula.[114] By 25 October 1950, Communist China entered the war on the side of North Korea with permission from the Soviet Union. As American forces maneuvered towards the Chinese border, the Chinese People's Volunteer Army attacked into North Korea and drove South Korean and American forces south of the 38th parallel.[115] During the remainder of 1950 and 1951, KMAG advisors continued to advise the remnants of the R.O.K. Army in its effort to halt the enemy offensive.

Prior to the North Korean invasion of South Korea in June 1950, the U.S. was not willing to invest fully in creating a competent and capable R.O.K. Army. KMAG advisors had willing counterparts that proved they could fight if manned and equipped properly, but U.S. foreign policy had limited KMAG's ability to expand and equip the R.O.K. Army. With ample funding and equipment, the R.O.K. Army had the potential to grow into a force capable of defeating North Korea. Throughout 1950-1951, remnants of the R.O.K. Army valiantly fought against North Korea. KMAG hastily reorganized the remnants of the R.O.K. Army into four divisions, and on 9 August 1950, received approval from Far East Command to grow the R.O.K. Army into a ten-division army. Major equipment shortfalls slowed KMAG's ability to expand the R.O.K.A. because equipment priority went to American units.[116] By July 1951, with fighting stabilized at the 38th Parallel, the Department of the Army asked the newly appointed Far East Commander, General Matthew Ridgway, for his estimate to make the R.O.K. Army effective. Interestingly, the U.S. Army was debating placing U.S. officers in charge of R.O.K. Army units without permission from the R.O.K. government, but General Ridgway blocked this effort.[117] In Ridgway's estimate to the Department of the Army, he recognized the need to develop a professional officer and non-commissioned officer corps instilled with an aggressive fighting spirit and the will to fight for their country. He sent the following recommendations to the Department of the Army:

1. The establishment of a replacement training and school command to supervise the R.O.K. Army's schooling and training
2. The establishment of a U.S. Army-type military reservation, and a centralization of R.O.K. Army training installations for the combat arms.
3. An increase in the number of US Army personnel at R.O.K. Army training installations.
4. An intensive leadership program for the R.O.K. Army.
5. An intensive leadership training program for the R.O.K. Army.
6. More training of R.O.K. officers in the U.S. Army service schools.
7. Pressure on the Republic of Korea Government to insure disciplinary measures against incompetent, corrupt, or cowardly R.O.K. officers and government officials.
8. A rehabilitation program for all R.O.K. infantry divisions.
9. The development of service units for a ten-division R.O.K. Army.
10. An increase in the number of automatic weapons, artillery, and tanks in the R.O.K. Army, as units demonstrated an ability to absorb and use additional equipment.[118]

General Ridgway recognized that the R.O.K. Army needed leadership and training if it were to improve, and placed this responsibility on Lieutenant General James Van Fleet. Van Fleet took command of the Eighth Army following General Ridgway's promotion to Far East Command and Supreme Allied Commander on 14 April 1951, and was essential in implementing R.O.K. Army reforms.[119] Van Fleet held unique qualifications that made him the right man to rebuild the R.O.K. Army into a capable military. Prior to assuming command, Van Fleet had commanded the U.S. Army Military Group – Greece, which trained and equipped the Greek military during the Greek Civil War from 1948 to 1949.[120] He had a gift for coordinating civil-military efforts, and had spent time working with the American Mission in Greece as a member of the Joint U.S. Military Advisory and Planning Group, an interagency under the control of the ambassador, developing initiatives for anti-communist Greek security forces. This experience proved essential to his efforts in Korea to rebuild the R.O.K. Army. Van Fleet had an amicable relationship with President Rhee, with whom he shared common interest in wanting to build a R.O.K. Army capable of defeating the communist North.[121] Immediately, Van Fleet met with South Korean political leadership, U.S. Army commanders, and R.O.K. Army leaders. During the meeting, he stated that R.O.K. Army competency was essential to the success of maintaining a sovereign South Korea.[122]

Lieutenant General Van Fleet brought in a new KMAG commander to oversee the advisory mission of the R.O.K. Army, Brigadier General Cornelius Ryan. Ryan brought with him a reputation of being a master trainer and getting the mission accomplished with finite resources while commanding the 101st Airborne Division (Training) at Camp Breckenridge, Kentucky.[123] Van Fleet gave Ryan two mandates to reform the R.O.K. Army: transform the South Korean Army into a fighting force capable of defeating North Korea and make the Korean Military Advisory Group responsive to the needs of the R.O.K. Army.[124] Remarkably, Van Fleet gave Ryan the ability to rebuild the R.O.K. Army by assigning the best replacement officers to KMAG.[125] Additionally, Ryan worked to improve the relationship between KMAG and the Eighth Army division commanders because he realized KMAG's success in battle depended upon American commanders' support to the R.O.K.A.[126]

From 1950 until 1953, KMAG continued to build and expand the R.O.K. Army into a fighting force able to deter the North Korean threat. An analysis of KMAG doctrine, organization, and training will facilitate an understanding of how the R.O.K.

Army transformed from 1950 to 1953, and will provide the current force a better appreciation of the intricacies involved with advising foreign forces in the future.

---

[1]Bruce Cumings, *The Origins of the Korean War, Vol. I, Liberation and the Emergence of Separate Regimes* (Princeton: Princeton University Press, 1981), 104-09. Franklin Roosevelt made such a commitment as early as 1 December 1943 in a joint statement with Winston Churchill and Chiang Kai-shek that ―the aforesaid three powers (Great Britain, United States, and China), mindful of the enslavement of the people of Korea, are determined that in due course Korea shall become free and independent."

[2]Peter Lowe, *The Origins of the Korean War* (London: Longman Group, 1986), 12. The Soviet Union declared war on Russia on 8 August 1945 in cooperation with the Allied Powers of World War II, capturing significant parts of Manchuria prior to the end of the war on 15 August 1945.

[3]Ibid., 14.

[4]Max Hastings, *The Korean War* (New York: Touchstone, 1987), 27.

[5]Lowe, *The Origins of the Korean War*, 14.

[6]Duncan Sinclair, ―Operations and Accomplishments," *Military Review* 27 (August 1947): 54.

[7]Lowe, *The Origins of the Korean War*, 14-15.

[8]Ibid., 12-14.

[9]Wilson Miscamble, *From Roosevelt to Truman: Potsdam, Hiroshima and the Cold War* (Cambridge: Cambridge University Press, 2007), 307-308.

[10]Hastings, *The Korean War*, 26, 44.

[11]Allan Millett, *The War For Korea: 1945-1950: A House Burning* (Lawrence: University Press of Kansas, 2005), 68.

[12]Hastings, *The Korean War*, 37.

[13]Ibid., 44.

[14]Ibid., 45.

[15]Cumings, *The Origins of the Korean War*, 35-36.

[16]Millett, *The War for Korea*, 105.

[17]Hastings, *The Korean War*, 38.

[18]Harry G. Huppert, ―Korean Occupational Problems,‖ *Military Review* 29 (December 1949): 11.

[19]Korean Institute of Military History, *The Korean War*, vol. I (Lincoln: University of Nebraska Press 2000-2001), 17-18.

[20]Ibid., 12.

[21]Millett, *The War for Korea*, 64-65.

[22]Ibid., 85.

[23]Bryan R. Gibby, ―Fighting in a Korean War: The American Advisory Missions from 1946-1953‖ (PhD diss., Ohio State University, 2004), 36. This dissertation is available online at http://etd.ohiolink.edu/view.cgi?acc%5Fnum=osu1086202227.

[24]Hastings, *The Korean War*, 27.

[25]Robert Sawyer, *Military Advisors in Korea: KMAG in Peace and War* (Washington, DC: Office of the Chief of Military History, 1962), 7-8.

[26]Sawyer, *Military Advisors in Korea*, 8.

[27]Ibid., 9.

[28]T. E. Lawrence, ―27 Articles,‖ *The Arab Bulletin, 1917*, http://wwi.lib.byu.edu/index.php/The_27_Articles_of_T.E._Lawrence (accessed 26 December 2010).

[29]Ibid., 9.

[30]Peter Clemens, ―Captain James Hausman, U.S. Army Military Advisor to Korea, 1946-48: The Intelligent Man on the Spot,‖ *Journal of Strategic Studies* 25, no. 1 (March 2002): 169.

[31]Sawyer, *Military Advisors in Korea*, 10.

[32]Ibid., 12.

[33]Ibid., 16.

[34]Millett, *The War for Korea*, 109.

[35]Andrew J. Birtle, ―The Korean Civil War, 1945-1954,‖ in *U.S. Army Counterinsurgency and Contingency Operations Doctrine 1942-1976* (Washington, DC: Center of Military History, 2003), 86.

[36] Ibid., 86.

[37] Allen Millett, *The Korean War* (Dulles: Potomac Books, 2007), 7.

[38] Millett, *The War for Korea*, 135.

[39] Ibid., 106.

[40] Sawyer, *Military Advisors in Korea*, 13-15.

[41] Ibid., 13.

[42] Ibid., 15.

[43] Ibid., 20-21.

[44] Millett, *The War for Korea*, 106.

[45] Korean Institute of Military History, *The Korean War*, Vol. I, 62-66.

[46] Sawyer, *Military Advisors in Korea*, 13-14.

[47] Gibby, "Fighting in a Korean War," 31.

[48] Clemens, "Captain James Hausman," 176. USAMGIK disbanded the English language school in late 1946 requiring all South Korean officers to earn their commission at the Korean Training Center.

[49] Ibid., 177.

[50] Sawyer, *Military Advisors in Korea*, 25.

[51] Allan Millett, "Captain James H. Hausman and the Formation of the Korean Army 1945-1950," *Armed Forces and Society* 23, no. 4 (1997): 511.

[52] Clemens, "Captain James Hausman," 170.

[53] Sawyer, *Military Advisors in Korea*, 23.

[54] Clemens, "Captain James Hausman," 2.

[55] Ibid., 172.

[56] Ibid., 173.

[57] Gibby, "Fighting in a Korean War," 40.

[58] Sawyer, *Military Advisors in Korea*, 32.

[59]Gibby, —Figling in a Korean War," 57.

[60]Sawyer, *Military Advisors in Korea*, 34-35.

[61]Ibid., 35.

[62]Gibby, —Figling in a Korean War," 57.

[63]Sawyer, *Military Advisors in Korea*, 41.

[64]Ibid., 36.

[65]Ibid., 37.

[66]Ibid., 38.

[67]Korean Institute of Military History, *The Korean War*, Vol. I, 32-33.

[68]Cumings, *The Origins of the Korean War*, 259.

[69]Ibid., 262.

[70]Sawyer, *Military Advisors in Korea*, 39-40.

[71]Cumings, *The Origins of the Korean War*, 264.

[72]Ibid., 264-265.

[73]Ibid., 264.

[74]Gibby, —Figling in a Korean War," 63.

[75]Sawyer, *Military Advisors in Korea*, 40.

[76]Gibby, —Figling in a Korean War," 64-65.

[77]Sawyer, *Military Advisors in Korea*, 40-41.

[78]Clemens, —Captain James Hausman," 181.

[79]Millett, *The War for Korea*, 172.

[80]Millett, —Captain James H. Hausman and the Formation of the Korean Army 1945-1950," 518.

[81]Sawyer, *Military Advisors in Korea*, 41.

[82]Ibid., 42-43.

[83]Ibid., 43.

[84]*Secretary of State to the Embassy in Korea Telegram, 1949, Foreign Relations of the United States*, http://images.library.wisc.edu/FRUS/EFacs/1949v07p2/M/0411.jpg (accessed 26 December 2010).

[85]Sawyer, *Military Advisors in Korea*, 44.

[86]Ibid., 45.

[87]Sawyer, *Military Advisors in Korea*, 57.

[88]Cumings, *The Origins of the Korean War*, 466-467.

[89]*Secretary of State to the Embassy in Korea Telegram.*

[90]Sawyer, *Military Advisors in Korea*, 112.

[91]Roy Appleman, *U.S. Army in the Korean War: South to the Naktong, North to the Yalu* (Washington, DC: Center of Military History, 1961), 8.

[92]Millett, *The War for Korea*, 240.

[93]Cumings, *The Origins of the Korean War*, 338.

[94]Millett, *The War for Korea*, 240.

[95]Appleman, *United States Army in Korea*, 18.

[96]Millett, *The War for Korea*, 249.

[97]Ibid., 251.

[98]Hastings, *The Korean War*, 52-53.

[99]Appleman, *U.S. Army in the Korean War*, 35.

[100]Jager, —Iraqi Security Forces and the Lessons from Korea," 212.

[101]Sawyer, *Military Advisors in Korea*, 140.

[102]Andreas Dorpalen, *The Cambridge History of Warfare* (New York: Cambridge University Press, 1995), 343.

[103]Hastings, *The Korean War*, 55-56.

[104]Dorpalen, *The Cambridge History of Warfare*, 343.

[105]Hastings, *The Korean War*, 59.

[106]Appleman, *U.S. Army in the Korean War*, 49-50.

[107]Callum A. MacDonald, *Korea, The War before Vietnam* (New York: The Free Press, 1987), 34-35.

[108]Appleman, *U.S. Army in the Korean War*, 51-53.

[109]Sawyer, *Military Advisors in Korea*, 118.

[110]Ibid., 124-125.

[111]Robert Ramsey, *Advising Indigenous Forces: American Advisors in Korea, Vietnam, and El Salvador* (Fort Leavenworth, KS: Combat Studies Institute Press, 2006), 6.

[112]Sawyer, *Military Advisors in Korea*, 118.

[113]Ibid., 146.

[114]Dorpalen, *The Cambridge History of Warfare*, 344.

[115]Chen Jian, *China's Road to the Korean War* (New York: Columbia University Press, 1994), 211-213.

[116]Sawyer, *Military Advisors in Korea*, 143-146.

[117]Ibid., 170-171.

[118]Ibid., 176.

[119]Paul Braim, *The Will to Win* (Annapolis: Naval Institute Press, 2001), 243.

[120]Ibid., 163.

[121]Ibid., 272.

[122]Ibid., 245.

[123]Gibby, —Fighting in a Korean War," 189.

[124]Ibid., 190.

[125]Braim, *The Will to Win*, 272-273.

[126]Ibid., 195.

CHAPTER 3

THE REBIRTH OF THE R.O.K. ARMY: 1950 TO 1953

On 25 June 1950, the NKPA invaded South Korea, thus delaying U.S. Army advisory initiatives to build a competent and capable R.O.K. Army. The onset of war multiplied personnel, training, leadership, and equipment requirements for the army, and destroyed the South Korean infrastructure that supported military development, making the task to rebuild the army that much harder.[1] By 15 July 1950, South Korean President Rhee Syngman, declared that R.O.K. Army forces were under direct command of the U.S. led United Nations Command.[2] It was now up to USAFIK, led by Eighth Army, to rebuild the R.O.K. Army. How did KMAG facilitate the transformation of the R.O.K. Army from 1950 to 1953 into a competent and capable institution able to deter North Korea and re-establish the sovereign territory of South Korea?

Doctrine

Military doctrine provides the foundation for building an army by identifying the ways and means to achieve military objectives. Military historian, Colonel J. F. C. Fuller noted that the —central idea of an army is known as its doctrine, which to be sound must be principles of war, and which to be effective must be elastic enough to admit of mutation in accordance with change in circumstance."[3] Additionally, current U.S. military publications define doctrine as the —fundamental principles by which the military forces or elements thereof guide their actions in support of national objectives. It is authoritative but requires judgment in application."[4] Doctrine establishes the intellectual framework military leaders use to change organizations.[5] Ultimately, doctrine guides the way militaries wage war.

Prior to the invasion of South Korea, KMAG advisors introduced U.S. style doctrine for use in operations and training, instead of using existing Japanese military doctrine. In fact, it was an early objective of KMAG's predecessor to extinguish Japanese doctrine from the fledgling R.O.K. Army. Implementing U.S. doctrine, however, proved difficult because the R.O.K. Army was illiterate in the Korean language and did not understand English.[6] Thus, all instruction was oral and a great deal of time was devoted to translating training through an interpreter, which took away valuable time from the actual training exercise.[7]

USAFIK and KMAG decided to implement U.S. style doctrine because advisors knew it, and were comfortable teaching it to Korean soldiers. New R.O.K. Army doctrine needed to be basic enough to implement in the fledgling R.O.K. Army, yet flexible enough to allow experienced Constabulary soldiers to conduct advanced level training. Interestingly, U.S. doctrine manuals were hard to come by and it took months for KMAG to receive copies from stateside institutions, such as the Infantry School at Fort Benning, Georgia.[8] Luckily, Major Eugene McDonald brought some literature with him on his KMAG assignment in 1949 that included the Mobilization Training Plan 7-1. Written in 1943, it was the training doctrine for U.S. infantry regiments during World War II. Beginning in 1949, the U.S. Army's Mobilization Training Plan 7-1 was the primary training document for the R.O.K. Army and remained in use until the army developed its own doctrine.[9] Its clear program of instruction, from the individual soldier to regimental level, made it ideal for the flexible training program required to train the R.O.K. Army.

Additionally, Mobilization Training Plan 7-1 called for a table of organization and equipment that mirrored the current light weapons and equipment configuration of the R.O.K. Army, because it did not require recently developed heavy weapons such as the recoilless rifle.[10] Moreover, as the R.O.K. Army expanded its table of organization, KMAG easily modified the plan, specifically as it pertained to augmenting the R.O.K. Army with heavier weapons and equipment later in the war.

Following the outbreak of war in June 1950, it became obvious that the R.O.K. Army had yet to grasp the key concept of combined arms operations contained in U.S. doctrine. The ROKA's lack of leadership, troop control, and firepower resulted from a lack of combined arms training and heavy equipment. These deficiencies allowed the NKPA to defeat R.O.K. Army defensive positions. Only American support to the R.O.K. Army thru aircraft and limited U.S. troop deployment to bolster R.O.K. defensive positions allowed the R.O.K. Army to conduct a fighting withdrawal and salvage remnants of its force.[11] Throughout July and August of 1950, KMAG advisors assumed command of R.O.K. Army units because any semblance of order and chain of command in the R.O.K. Army had dissolved.[12]

After the invasion, KMAG continued to use the same training doctrine to train the R.O.K. Army that was in use before the war. Because most R.O.K. Army soldiers were illiterate, KMAG advisors developed visual training aids that conveyed the tasks, conditions, and standards for training without relying on written material.[13] Additionally, the new KMAG Commander, Brigadier General Ryan, pushed to make the training doctrine more accessible to Korean officers, who were literate, by translating U.S. doctrine into the Korean language. Moreover, translated training documents enabled

R.O.K. Army leaders to conduct their own training rather than rely on advisors. Additionally, KMAG advisors could monitor and evaluate R.O.K. Army officers quicker by observing their leadership skills during training, and if necessary recommend their removal for incompetence prior to combat.[14]

In addition to implementing and improving doctrine for the R.O.K. Army, KMAG continued to develop advisor doctrine to assist KMAG advisors in training and mentoring the R.O.K. Army. In 1951, Brigadier General Ryan published a new advisor handbook that expanded earlier R.O.K. Army training guidance. This new version consolidated KMAG operational procedures including mission, objectives, organizational structure, and procedures covering administration, supply, and interpreter services. Additionally, it provided technical guidance that outlined advisor duties and responsibilities. It also listed reporting procedures and guidance on the internal supply process. Most importantly, the final section of the handbook described the KMAG Commanders vision for the organization and suggestions for unit advisors. These suggestions focused on the basic functions of advisory work such as understanding the mission and the people, for gaining the confidence and respect of the Korean officers and troops, personal involvement with the Korean unit, and situational awareness.[15] The handbook stressed that advisors were not commanders, but that they should operate as if they were commanding the R.O.K. Army. The handbook offered tips for building counterpart rapport, unmentioned in previous versions, and mainly focused on the use of combat enablers such as fire support and aircraft to gain the trust of counterparts. The new edition of the KMAG Handbook placed the success of the R.O.K. Army on the shoulders of KMAG advisors. In many ways, the new handbook increased advisor responsibility for R.O.K. Army conduct, and limited the development of an independent and self-sufficient R.O.K. Army.[16]

Organization

In June 1950, the R.O.K. Army had constabulary roots and was a force incapable of major combat operations.[17] R.O.K. Army units were capable of conducting counterinsurgency operations, but unable to handle an offensive oriented NKPA capable of combined arms maneuver.[18] On 25 June 1950, R.O.K. Army units faced their first battle against the Russian made T-34 tank of the NKPA without the weapons to repel them. Within days, the R.O.K. Army fell back south of the Han River, with half of the eight R.O.K. Army divisions unaccounted for, and with only thirty percent of its assigned weapons.[19] Clearly, the U.S. Army needed to re-focus efforts on expanding and equipping the R.O.K. Army.

Based on a staff study conducted on 17 July 1950, General MacArthur's Far East Command initially recommended rebuilding the pre-war R.O.K. Army. Eighth Army Commander, General Walker, and Ambassador Muccio strongly opposed the staff study's findings, and continued to push for R.O.K. Army expansion. Full mobilization of South Korea meant the U.S. would not have to commit large numbers of ground troops.[20] Their appeal influenced General MacArthur to approve R.O.K. Army expansion on 9 August 1950.[21] Thus, the R.O.K. Army expanded to a ten-division army based on the Tables of Distribution and Allowance for a U.S. Army division from 1942.[22] Despite expansion, the R.O.K. Army continued to lack the heavy weapons necessary to destroy NKPA tanks.

Interestingly, as new R.O.K. Army divisions grew, a new personnel program started that is still in use in South Korea today. As the U.S. prepared to conduct major combat operations against North Korea, it was woefully short of personnel in U.S. combat divisions due to casualties. In response to this, MacArthur assigned 500 out of every 2,950 R.O.K. Army replacements to U.S. front line combat units.[23] This program, the Korean Augmentation to the US Army, commonly referred to as KATUSA, continued throughout the duration of the war, and is still in use today in South Korea.[24] A benefit of this program was R.O.K. Army soldier immersion into the customs and doctrine of the U.S. Army. When KATUSAs rotated back to R.O.K. Army units they took with them an appreciation for the American way of waging war, and influenced the R.O.K. Army to adopt the technology and systems that made the U.S. Army successful.[25]

In the beginning of the war, the State Department mission in Korea directly controlled KMAG. On 15 July 1950, General MacArthur and the Far East Command task organized the R.O.K. Army and KMAG directly under Eighth Army command allowing them to have direct control of R.O.K. Army units and advisory functions in South Korea.[26] Additionally, on 26 September 1950, the U.S. Army increased authorized KMAG advisor strength from 500 personnel to 835 personnel. This new KMAG task organization was a direct reflection of its R.O.K. Army counterpart, and provided an advisor to every commander down to regimental level and battalion level in combat arms and combat support units.[27] The new structure facilitated the advisory relationship necessary to mentor and develop R.O.K. Army leaders and their staffs. Once General Van Fleet assumed control of Eighth Army on 14 April 1951, he worked diligently to define the awkward command relationship between Eighth Army and KMAG to synchronize the advisory mission.

Furthermore, KMAG created a deputy commander position to assist with command and control of R.O.K. Army Training. This deputy commander position allowed the KMAG Commander, Brigadier General Ryan, to concentrate his efforts on advising the R.O.K. Army Chief of Staff, and to work on initiatives supporting the advisory mission. Brigadier General Thomas Cross became the KMAG deputy commander responsible for the newly designated Field Training Command. He ensured R.O.K. Army units conducted comprehensive field training exercises to prepare them for combat.[28] Subsequently, the Eighth Army's new commander, Lieutenant General Van Fleet, instructed U.S. Corps commanders to conduct R.O.K. Army re-training in the rear areas. In fact, Lieutenant General Van Fleet took a risk by pulling R.O.K. Army Units for re-training as the fighting with North Korea lulled in 1951. This allowed R.O.K. Army units to rotate off the front line and concentrate on re-training with the support of KMAG. The Field Training Command accomplished R.O.K. Army re-training through direct coordination with U.S. Corps commanders in rear area designated regional training centers.

Eighth Army and KMAG needed an expansion plan for the R.O.K. Army that covered officer training and education, tactical training, and increased lethality on the battlefield.[29] Immediately after Lieutenant General Van Fleet assumed duties as the Eighth Army Commander he emphasized R.O.K. Army leadership as the biggest reason for its failure in combat. Moreover, many of the R.O.K. Army generals were new to senior command positions, having been promoted only recently from lieutenant or captain.[30] Lieutenant General Van Fleet worked tirelessly with R.O.K. Army divisions to evaluate and identify future R.O.K. Army leaders. He understood the importance of KMAG in improving the R.O.K. Army and continued to push for the organization to grow. The new Far East Commander, General Ridgway supported his efforts to expand KMAG and the organization grew to 1,055 personnel by 15 August 1951.[31] In order to improve the leadership in the R.O.K. Army, Van Fleet sought to assign only the best replacement officers for service in KMAG. It was his desire to assign only the most combat-hardened Eighth Army veterans to the advisory mission.[32] However, he never fulfilled this. Personnel records from Eighth Army show that 81 percent of KMAG advisors were from the Army's reserve component, highlighting the problem KMAG had in attracting experienced active duty soldiers to the advisory mission.[33]

Additionally, Lieutenant General Van Fleet equipped the R.O.K Army with better weapons to fight the NKPA. Prior to this initiative, NKPA equipment outmatched the R.O.K. Army. Pre-war advisory initiatives supplied the R.O.K. Army with light weapons useful primarily for conducting policing actions and counterinsurgency operations, while the Soviets equipped the NKPA with the latest T-34 tank, and large amounts of artillery. Moreover, before the North Korean attack, American policy makers in Washington refused to consider appeals for better R.O.K. Army equipment by the U.S. Embassy and the R.O.K. Government because of budgetary constraints and a focus on domestic policies.[34] The outbreak of war brought the realization that the R.O.K. Army needed proper equipment to wage war against the NKPA. Significantly, Lieutenant General Van Fleet partnered with R.O.K. President Rhee Syngman to outfit the R.O.K. Army for major combat operations.[35] Notably, the increase the quantity and quality of equipment the R.O.K. Army received from the U.S. required KMAG to institute accountability procedures in the R.O.K. Army. Black marketeering and lack of equipment maintenance ran rampant throughout the R.O.K. Army, and it required significant effort by KMAG to institute equipment and supply discipline in R.O.K. Army organizations.[36]

KMAG continued re-training R.O.K. Army units in accordance with Lieutenant General Van Fleet's guidance, and on 23 June 1951 received welcome, yet unexpected, news. The Soviet Union began expressing interest in peace talks between North and South Korea. These peace talks slowed the fighting between North and South Korea and bought valuable time for the Eighth Army and KMAG to prepare the R.O.K. Army to take the lead in defense of South Korea.[37] During the remainder of 1951, the peace talks stalled, and Eighth Army continued limited offensive operations against the NKPA, creating a buffer zone along the 38th Parallel that allowed additional R.O.K. Army units to re-train.[38]

By September 1952, Lieutenant General Van Fleet and KMAG brought sweeping changes to the R.O.K. Army through their training initiatives. At the same time, American policy focused on turning the war over to the R.O.K. government.[39] Far East Command, led by General Ridgway, limited Eighth Army's ability to conduct large-scale offensive operations because a cease-fire seemed imminent between North and South Korea. For the first time, General Ridgway recognized the creation of a robust and effective R.O.K. Army as an objective of his command. Thus, Lieutenant General Van Fleet received permission to assign limited numbers of senior experienced officers to KMAG to support training of the R.O.K. Army. At the same time, young R.O.K. Army officers also began emerging as capable leaders forged in combat. Specifically, Lee

Chong-Chan and Paik Sun-Yup, each of whom were future R.O.K. Army Chiefs of Staff. However, the massive R.O.K. Army re-training program was seriously tested in the fall of 1952 by the NKPA."[40]

By 1952, KMAG grew to over 2000 personnel but the R.O.K. Army still struggled to field ten full infantry divisions.[41] Efforts were set in place to complete the R.O.K. Army re-organization and re-building plan by the end of 1952. Regardless of the efforts made by KMAG to rebuild the R.O.K. Army, American and South Korean Government officials continued to debate the ultimate size of the R.O.K. Army. In January 1952, the U.S. Secretary of Defense recommended that the R.O.K. Army remain at 250,000 personnel, organized into ten divisions. South Korean President Rhee and Lieutenant General Van Fleet argued that ten divisions were not enough to defend South Korea after the war, and recommended creating an additional ten R.O.K. Army divisions for defensive purposes.[42] American policy makers and Far East Command continued to limit further expansion of the R.O.K. Army, but did increase the size of the R.O.K. Army Service Corps to 60,000 personnel, thus greatly increasing the R.O.K. Army's staying power and ability to support units in combat.[43]

In May 1952, General Mark Clark succeeded General Ridgeway as commander of the U.S. led United Nations Command. General Clark, like Lieutenant General Van Fleet, supported the creation of a larger R.O.K. Army able to defeat the North Korean People's Army. He successfully advocated for the expansion of the ROKA, and instituted an increase in the number of armor and artillery units, making the R.O.K. Army capable of holding its own against the NKPA.[44] By the fall of 1952, the R.O.K. Army had acquired sixteen battalions of 105mm howitzer artillery, six battalions of 155mm howitzer artillery, and four companies of tanks. The R.O.K. Army continued to equip and train heavy weapons units until each of the twenty R.O.K. Army divisions had a battalion of artillery and a company of tanks in direct support of combat operations.[45]

The NKPA resumed major combat offensives against the United Nations Command from September 1952 to December 1953.[46] KMAG assisted R.O.K. Army units fought valiantly and established themselves as a combat capable military. Additionally, R.O.K. Army size continued to grow from 376,000 personnel in 1952 to over 576,000 personnel in 1953. This increase also led to an increase in KMAG advisors to 2,866 personnel by the end of the war.[47] KMAG continued to advise the R.O.K. Army as fighting stalled in July 1953, ultimately leading to a cease-fire agreement on 27 July 1953.[48] As part of the cease-fire agreement, South Korean President Rhee Syngman successfully negotiated for continued U.S. support of the R.O.K. Army.[49]

Training

The R.O.K. Army of 1949 was not a military force capable of conducting operations above the platoon level. Initial KMAG inspections of units noted that most units had completed multiple cycles of basic training, but had little experience at anything above platoon level. Even basic soldier skills, such as marksmanship, were missing due to a lack of leadership, training, and discipline. In spite of these deficiencies, the R.O.K. soldiers had nationalistic pride that brought extreme levels of high morale to their formations. Colonel Don MacDonald, an early KMAG advisor, remarked that the R.O.K. Army of 1949 —coud have been the American Army of 1775."[50] Additionally, the R.O.K. Army had little ability to sustain itself in combat, and sufficient numbers of training facilities did not exist to train the ever-expanding R.O.K.A. After the war began on 25

June 1950, however, KMAG aggressively developed a training program to pull R.O.K. Army divisions from the line and retrain them for four weeks.[51] A cornerstone of the retraining program was its incorporation of tactics, techniques, and procedures gathered from the battlefields of Korea. KMAG advisors did an exceptional job of capturing and sharing relevant combat tactics amongst each other that enabled combat-focused R.O.K. Army re-training. Significantly, the KMAG Handbook became the mechanism by which advisors shared relevant tactics, techniques, and procedures across the organization.[52] This effort, spurred by the KMAG Commander, caused an increase in training efficiency throughout the R.O.K. Army, but it still did not address how to increase the quality or training of KMAG advisors.

Even after the war started, advisor training did not improve. Through 1953, training still consisted of a KMAG orientation and issuance of the handbook. KMAG and the Eighth Army established no further advisor training initiatives throughout the war. KMAG after-action reviews highlighted the need for additional advisory training, but the U.S. Army did not pursue further training initiatives. Effectively, this meant that different R.O.K. Army units achieved different readiness rates based on advisory competence.[53] Despite this, the KMAG Commander continued to try to assign quality advisors to implement training reform of the R.O.K. Army. He insisted that advisors have combat experience, but did not discriminate against reservists because they formed the majority of KMAG replacements. Instead, he employed reservists in positions maximizing their mixture of military and civilian experience, which proved valuable in a mission that necessitated a wide array of skills.[54] Additionally, Lieutenant General Van Fleet supported Brigadier General Ryan by assigning successful Eighth Army battalion and regimental commanders as advisors to instill leadership in the R.O.K. Army. He attempted to dissolve the negative stigma of advisory duty by emphasizing assignment to KMAG over U.S. Army command positions, but many senior officers still had their assignments diverted to other billets because they did not understand the strategic impact of the mission.[55]

Brigadier General Ryan brought a fresh attitude to the organization of KMAG through his understanding of the requirement to build rapport with R.O.K. Army counterparts. As an example to all members of KMAG, Brigadier General Ryan travelled with the R.O.K Army Chief of Staff at all times to enhance rapport with his counterpart. As he travelled across the organization, he stressed the importance of establishing relationships with their South Korean counterparts to the men of KMAG. Clearly, Ryan's emphasis on rapport building worked because KMAG advisors developed multiple techniques to establish relationships and trust with their counterparts. Some advisors exercised patience and observed their counterpart from afar for as long as three weeks, before they stepped in to provide guidance. Other KMAG advisors found it best to offer advice only when asked by their R.O.K. Army counterpart. In each case, these KMAG advisors focused on forming relationships with their counterparts and gaining the confidence of the R.O.K. Army.[56] No studies exist to highlight what technique worked best, but Alfred Hausrath's survey of KMAG officers after the war acknowledges the importance of gaining counterpart trust and rapport.[57] Despite Ryan's emphasis on building bonds with the R.O.K.A., some KMAG advisors ignored forming relationships with counterparts and imposed changes in the R.O.K.A. in a typical U.S. Army officer authoritarian fashion.

KMAG created an elaborate training program prior to the war with North Korea, but the NKPA invasion destroyed the institutions established before the war. Additionally, Eighth Army could no longer afford to divert the personnel and resources to build a large training network due to the war effort. Instead, it used valuable experience from pre-war efforts to build an effective smaller training system in a short amount of time.[58] As the war began to stabilize along the 38th Parallel in 1951, American leadership in Washington and Far East Command re-emphasized improving the effectiveness of the R.O.K. Army.[59] U.S. military leaders recognized the R.O.K. Army as strategically important for the defense of South Korea, and a way to facilitate the withdrawal of U.S. combat forces.[60] The first step to fielding an improved R.O.K. Army was to re-establish the training system. Brigadier General Ryan increased advisory personnel allowing KMAG to staff new training institution initiatives. As KMAG advisory strength grew between 1951 and 1953, it allowed the command to staff R.O.K. Army training institutions with advisors, and to maintain advisory presence in line units.[61]

The first training institution to re-open was a combined arms officer training facility at Tongnae on 28 August 1950, which provided an eight-week course of instruction.[62] By early 1951, KMAG consolidated infantry, field artillery, and signal training for R.O.K. Army recruits at Kwangju in Southwest Korea. This new facility, called the Korean Army Training Center, provided the ability to train up to 15,000 troops at a time.[63] Additionally, all South Korean officer candidate schools, modeled after the U.S. officer candidate school program, increased instruction from eighteen to twenty-four weeks to increase the war fighting skills of future company grade officers. Significantly, the R.O.K. Army established the Korean Military Academy at Chinhae, showing long-term interest in creating a professional officer corps. Patterned after West Point, this institution offered a full, four-year curriculum to train capable officers for the R.O.K. Army. In order to provide mid-level field grade officers to units in combat, KMAG established a Command and General Staff School at Taegu, modeled after the US Army Command and General Staff School at Fort Leavenworth, Kansas. Additionally, the U.S. Army approved sending 250 R.O.K. Army officers annually to U.S. Army schools in late 1951, providing immersion in U.S. doctrine and training techniques that graduates took back to R.O.K. Army formations.[64] As R.O.K. Army schools re-opened, KMAGs increased authorization for advisors from 1951-1953 facilitated the staffing of all R.O.K. Army training institutions with advisory support.

All of these measures addressed shortcomings in R.O.K. Army leadership. As stated above, KMAG developed a R.O.K. Army officer training apparatus that modeled its program of instruction on the U.S. officer-training model. KMAG trained a corps of junior officers that had double the combat training as its pre-war counterpart. Additionally, each of these young officers shared common doctrine, and was meticulously prepared for their duties in combat. By 1953, KMAG had trained over 31,000 R.O.K. Army officers and prepared them to battle the NKPA.[65]

Starting in November 1951, combat support specialists such as quartermaster, transportation, intelligence, and medical services received additional emphasis. KMAG established support-training centers to staff the Korean Service Corps because it wanted to free up infantryman to fight the war, and it could only do this by relieving them of support tasks.[66] Additionally, such training provided the R.O.K. Army freedom to support its own operations and establish itself as an autonomous military force. Previously it relied upon KMAG advisors to handle support functions, but by 1952, the R.O.K. Army was becoming self-sufficient.

Most soldiers in the R.O.K. Army received little training prior to being committed to defensive operations against the NKPA. In fact, a majority of soldiers went straight from the recruit center to the front lines because of the necessity to guard the perimeter from NKPA assaults. Consequently, KMAG established the Field Training Command to re-train R.O.K. Army units operating on the Eighth Army defensive perimeter. This program required R.O.K. Army commanders to pull units from the defensive perimeter to concentrate on individual and collective military tasks. With the defense of the 38th Parallel stabilized during the summer of 1951, KMAG instituted this R.O.K. army re-training initiative.[67]

The Field Training Command program involved a two-month refresher-training program, during which time a R.O.K. Army division rotated off the front line to a regional training center near its area of operation. Each R.O.K. Army division conducted a three-phased program to improve their readiness and training levels. During phase one, KMAG assisted the division with equipment refit, and developed training schedules for the subsequent phases. This phase allowed KMAG to teach R.O.K.A. leaders how to conduct their own training. Phase two was a six-week refresher-training block that covered all facets of individual soldier skills, such as marksmanship, and occupation specific skills such as infantry, armor, and artillery core competencies. Throughout the six weeks of training, it progressed to collective level platoon and company level exercises. The third phase involved combined arms live fire battalion-level exercises combined with leadership and staff focused command post exercises. All training was as realistic as possible with live ammunition and night training. Additionally, combat support personnel received specialized training throughout the program to further their skills. Furthermore, KMAG had to certify that all units were proficient prior to their deployment back to the front lines.[68] R.O.K. Army General Paik Sun-Yup claimed that this re-training effort did more for the R.O.K. Army than any other U.S. initiative by increasing the capability and morale of South Korean soldiers.[69]

In addition to the training Field Training Command conducted at regional training centers, KMAG established the Korean Army Training Center at Kwangju. This facility had the ability to train R.O.K. Army recruits basic soldier tasks. Additionally, division sized units trained combined arms maneuver warfare at the Korean Army Training Center. The Korean Army Training Center featured heated classrooms, modern barracks, and dining facilities that became the pride of South Koreans. President Rhee dubbed it the —Home of the Nation's Warriors." The construction of the Korean Army Training Center brought pride and first class training to the R.O.K. Army, and by 1953, all R.O.K. Army units had rotated through two months of realistic combat training that emphasized U.S. style combined arms maneuver warfare.[70]

As KMAG began to solve the R.O.K. Army training issue, the U.S. Army advisory mission faced another problem affecting R.O.K. Army performance. How would KMAG solve the R.O.K. Army recruit induction and reception process problem, and facilitate trainees' movement into the training pipeline? This problem threatened R.O.K. Army readiness and its ability to staff the military. Prior to the war, and until reform, the R.O.K.A. recruited soldiers at the local level and transferred them to the Recruit Training Center. The local Regional In-processing Center gathered recruits from the countryside and quickly shipped them to the Recruit Training Center for initial military training without screening them. New recruits did not receive physical and mental screening until they reached the Recruit Training Center. Up to 25 percent of personnel failed screenings and 35 percent of personnel tested positive for tuberculosis, which adversely affected unit readiness rates. Subsequently, the KMAG Commander, Brigadier General Ryan, ordered a commission to develop solutions to the reception problem. By 1952, KMAG began to augment the Regional In-processing Centers with additional R.O.K. Army support personnel and advisors. The new process allowed the R.O.K. Army to pre-screen individuals prior to movement to Recruit Training Centers which improved the failure rate to less than 10 percent.[71]

Once KMAG solved the reception issue, another personnel problem involving recruits festered. As the R.O.K. Army expanded in 1952, training centers were reaching housing capacity. The first R.O.K. Army Recruit Training Center on Cheju Do Island could no longer house and feed the 15,000 new soldiers that in-processed annually. When that population grew to 28,000 between August and December 1952, the shortage of housing and food became a disaster for Eighth Army and KMAG. Lieutenant General Van Fleet stepped in quickly and authorized funding to increase the capacity of the first Recruit Training Center. Additionally, he allocated resources to build and staff a second Recruit Training Center in Nonsan for training combat support personnel, which relieved stress on the first Recruit Training Center.[72]

Training efforts continued to blossom and R.O.K. Army officers began to improve their organization with unique indigenous solutions. R.O.K. Army Chief of Staff, General Paik Sun-Yup, recognized that his army could not feed itself and faced a ration crisis. He worked diligently with KMAG to develop a central procurement agency, modeled after the U.S. Army's system. Korean Service Corps personnel received training in procurement and developed a system to draw produce from the local South Korean economy.[73] General Paik Sun-Yup's leadership served as a model for all R.O.K. officers as he pushed aggressively to develop the R.O.K. Army into a self-sufficient military force. By the cease-fire in July 1953, R.O.K. Army officers at all echelons had taken the lead in running R.O.K. Army training initiatives and defending South Korea.[74]

From 1950-1953 KMAG focused on rebuilding the R.O.K. Army and supported Eighth Army's efforts to defeat the NKPA. Through the evolution of doctrine, organization, and training the R.O.K. Army grew into a well-trained, heavily equipped, and capable army. KMAG's efforts in supporting the R.O.K. Army represent the first large scale U.S. advisory mission to form, build, and equip a foreign army.[75] Is KMAG's experience applicable to modern military advisory missions?

---

[1]Alfred Hausrath, *The KMAG Advisor: Role and Problems of the Military Advisor in Developing an Indigenous Army for Combat Operations in Korea* (Chevy Chase, MD: Operational Research Office, Johns Hopkins University, 1957), 1-2.

[2]Mark Clark, *From the Danube to the Yalu* (New York: Harper's Publishers, 1954), 169.

[3]J. F. C. Fuller, *The Foundations of the Science of War* (Fort Leavenworth, KS: U.S. Army Command and General Staff College Press, 1993), 254. Reprinted from the original 1926 edition.

[4]Joint Chiefs of Staff, Joint Publication 1-02, *Department of Defense Dictionary of Military and Related Terms* (Washington, DC: Government Printing Office, November 2010), 114, http://www.dtic.mil/doctrine/new_pubs/jp1_02.pdf (accessed 18 March 2011).

[5]David Cloud and Greg Jaffe, *The Fourth Star* (New York: Crown Publishers, 2009), 217.

[6]Bryan R. Gibby, ―Fighting in a Korean War: The American Advisory Missions from 1946-1953" (PhD diss., Ohio State University, 2004), 41. This dissertation is available online at http://etd.ohiolink.edu/view.cgi?acc%5Fnum=osu1086202227.

[7]Hausrath, *The KMAG Advisor,* 45-46, 67-68.

[8]Robert Sawyer, *Military Advisors in Korea: KMAG in Peace and War* (Washington: Office of the Chief of Military History, 1962), 70.

[9]Ibid.

[10]Ibid.

[11]Paik Sun-Yup, *From Pusan to Panmunjom* (McLean: Brassey's, 1992), 23-24.

[12]Sawyer, *Military Advisors in Korea,* 140.

[13]Gibby, ―Fighting in a Korean War," 41.

[14]Ibid., 196.

[15]Eighth U.S. Army, *KMAG Handbook* (Eighth Army Publishing Directorate, 1951), 42.

[16]Gibby, ―Fighting in a Korean War," 167.

[17]Sawyer, *Military Advisors in Korea,* 11.

[18]Roy Appleman, *U.S. Army in the Korean War: South to the Naktong, North to the Yalu* (Washington DC: Center of Military History, 1961), 17.

[19]Ibid., 34-35.

[20]Sawyer, *Military Advisors in Korea,* 145.

[21]Ibid., 145.

[22]Ibid., 146.

[23]Ibid., 149-150.

[24]David Skaggs, ―The Katusa Experiment: The Integration of Korean Nationals into the U.S. Army, 1950-1965." *Military Affairs* 38, no. 2 (April 1974): 53-55.

[25]Clark, *From the Danube to the Yalu,* 181.

[26]Sawyer, *Military Advisors in Korea,* 155; Mark Clark, *From the Danube to the Yalu* (New York: Harper's Publishers, 1954), 169.

[27]Sawyer, *Military Advisors in Korea*, 155.

[28]Gibby, —Fighing in a Korean War," 213.

[29]Ibid., 183.

[30]Paul Braim, *The Will to Win* (Annapolis: Naval Institute Press, 2001), 272.

[31]Sawyer, *Military Advisors in Korea*, 164.

[32]Braim, *The Will to Win*, 273.

[33]Hausrath, *The KMAG Advisor*, 109.

[34]Allan Millett, *The War For Korea: 1945-1950: A House Burning* (Lawrence: University Press of Kansas, 2005), 217.

[35]Braim, *The Will to Win*, 310.

[36]Hausrath, *The KMAG Advisor*, 67.

[37]Burton Kaufman, *The Korean War: Challenges in Crisis, Credibility, and Command* (New York: Alfred A. Knopf, 1986), 190-192.

[38]Callum A. MacDonald, *Korea, The War before Vietnam* (New York: The Free Press, 1987), 117-119.

[39]Ibid., 129-30.

[40]Gibby, —Fighing in a Korean War," 188.

[41]Robert Ramsey, *Advising Indigenous Forces: American Advisors in Korea, Vietnam, and El Salvador* (Fort Leavenworth, KS: Combat Studies Institute Press, 2006), 10.

[42]Walter G. Hermes, *Truce Tent and Fighting Front* (Washington, DC: U.S. Government Printing Office, 1966), 211.

[43]Sawyer, *Military Advisors in Korea*, 182.

[44]Hermes, *Truce Tent and Fighting Front*, 340.

[45]Sawyer, *Military Advisors in Korea*, 183-184.

[46]Gibby, —Fighing in a Korean War," 221.

[47]Ramsey, *Advising Indigenous Forces*, 10.

[48]MacDonald, *Korea, The War before Vietnam*, 198.

[49]Ibid., 195-196.

[50]Sawyer, *Military Advisors in Korea*, 69.

[51]Ibid., 140.

[52]Eighth U.S. Army, *KMAG Handbook* (Eighth Army Publishing Directorate, 1951), I.

[53]Ramsey, *Advising Indigenous Forces*, 13.

[54]Hausrath, *The KMAG Advisor*, 109.

[55]Gibby, —Fighting in a Korean War," 193.

[56]Ibid., 191.

[57]Hausrath, *The KMAG Advisor*, 43, 58-66.

[58]Sawyer, *Military Advisors in Korea*, 150-151.

[59]Hermes, *Truce Tent and Fighting Front*, 208.

[60]Ibid., 207.

[61]Sawyer, *Military Advisors in Korea*, 163.

[62] Ibid., 151.

[63] Ibid., 179.

[64]Ibid., 179-181.

[65]Hausrath, *The KMAG Advisor*, 44.

[66]Sawyer, *Military Advisors in Korea*, 182.

[67]Ibid., 181.

[68]Gibby, —Fighting in a Korean War," 214.

[69]Sun-Yup, *From Pusan to Panmunjom*, 162.

[70]Ibid., 235.

[71]Gibby, —Fighting in a Korean War," 210-211.

[72]Ibid., 206.

[73]Sun-Yup, *From Pusan to Panmunjom*, 209-210.

[74]Sawyer, *Military Advisors in Korea*, 188.

[75]Sheila Jager, —Iraqi Security Forces and Lessons from Korea," *Strategic Studies Institute Editorial* (December 2006): 211.

CHAPTER 4

SOUTH KOREA AND IRAQ: SECURITY FORCE ASSISTANCE

Since the terrorist attacks against America on 11 September 2001, the United States of America has been at war with violent extremist organizations to defeat their ability to threaten the nation's security.[1] This complex type of war combines diplomatic, economic, and military power to protect the national interests of the United States. This war requires the U.S. Army to train and operate with host nation security forces. In particular, the Iraq advisory mission to train a new Iraqi Army is mature, with advisory operations since the fall of 2003. Comparing U.S. Army advisory missions to build and train the new Iraqi Army with the efforts of KMAG to build and train a R.O.K. Army fifty years ago may spark debate on how to conduct future Security Force Assistance missions. Before any direct comparisons between Iraq and South Korea are possible, it is necessary to summarize the Iraq advisory mission to build a new Iraqi Army.

The Evolution of the U.S. Military Advisory Mission in Iraq

U.S. led coalition forces began major combat operations to defeat Saddam Hussein's Iraqi military on 19 March 2003, and in the span of three weeks, they effectively defeated the Iraqi military and dissolved the Baathist Regime. While the U.S - led coalition military operations were successful, U.S. policy planners did very little to prepare for operations following the defeat of Saddam Hussein.[2] After the culmination of major combat operations, General John Abizaid replaced General Tommy Franks at Central Command, the geographical combatant command responsible for the war. General John Abizaid maintained overall responsibility for Iraq, but relied on the

Pentagon's under-staffed and under-funded Office of Reconstruction and Humanitarian Assistance to rebuild the country following the war.[3] To complicate the post-conflict reconstruction effort further, the transitional Iraqi government, dubbed the Coalition Provisional Authority, replaced the Office of Reconstruction and Humanitarian Assistance on 11 May 2003. The Coalition Provisional Authority dumbfounded military planners as it immediately dissolved the Iraqi Military as part of Washington's de-Baathifaction effort. Significantly, Central Command military planners recognized the urgent need to rebuild Iraqi Army and police forces as early as June 2003, coinciding with the Coalition Provisional Authority decision to disband the Iraqi Military.[4]

At the conclusion of combat operations, the U.S. military designated V Corps as the war-fighting headquarters in charge of day-to-day affairs in Iraq, with Lieutenant General Ricardo Sanchez as the Corps Commander. This headquarters replaced the Coalition Land Force Component Command that executed the operational command and control of the war. In retrospect, the decision to change a corps headquarters into an operational command proved troublesome. The corps headquarters did not have sufficient staff or subject matter expertise to transition from a tactical to operational level headquarters.[5]

Throughout the summer of 2003, units under General Sanchez's command occupied permanent locations throughout Iraq in an effort to stabilize the country. At the same time, an insurgency developed in Iraq, led by foreign fighters influenced by Osama Bin Laden, former regime loyalists fighting for Saddam Hussein, and Iranian backed Shiite Muslims. Interestingly, the U.S. administration did not want to recognize the insurgency, and only accepted it as such once General Abizaid mentioned the insurgency in an international media interview.[6]

Initial efforts to rebuild the Iraqi military were paltry and lacked synchronization. Congress nominated Major General Paul Eaton in June 2003 to head the Coalition Military Assistance Training Team in an effort to rebuild the Iraqi Army from scratch. Initial estimates called for a force of 40,000 personnel, mainly focused on external security efforts to protect Iraq from neighboring countries.[7] This initial effort focused on using civilian contractors, mostly former service members, to train the Iraqi Army. Moreover, military planners failed to account for the force size necessary to deal with a growing insurgency. These initial Iraqi Army units lacked training and dissolved immediately once engaged in combat operations in Fallujah in April 2004.[8]

Simultaneous to the creation of a new Iraqi Army, U.S. ground commanders realized they needed additional forces to help stabilize the country and assist with security at the local level. This led to the creation of the Iraq Civil Defense Corps, later spawning the Iraqi National Guard, which resembled more of a constabulary than an army. All Iraq Civil Defense Corps training relied heavily on the initiative of individual U.S. battalion and brigade commanders. It was not a national program, was very decentralized, and received very little in resources and funding from the national level.[9] As the program caught on, the Coalition Military Assistance Training Team used the Iraqi Civil Defense Corps, and later the Iraqi National Guard, to bolster Iraqi Security Force numbers required to secure the population.[10] This discombobulated training effort did not produce high quality recruits, thus forcing the U.S. to abandon it. As the U.S.

abandoned the program, it transitioned some of the Iraqi National Guard units into regular army units on 6 July 2005.[11]

American efforts to restore and stabilize Iraq were shaky, at best, in late 2003. In an effort to bring unity of command to Iraq and implement a long-term counterinsurgency strategy, the U.S. Army established Multi-National Force Iraq in July 2004, headed by General George Casey. This coincided with American efforts to synchronize the restoration of the Iraqi Army with the creation of Multi-National Security Transition Command Iraq in June 2004, headed by Lieutenant General David Petraeus. The chain of command now existed in theater to stabilize the country, begin restoration, and focus on rebuilding the Iraqi Army. Multi-National Force Iraq synchronized combat operations and advisory operations through Multi-National Corps Iraq and Multi-National Security Transition Command Iraq, respectively.[12]

Multi-National Force Iraq transferred two billion dollars from the Iraqi infrastructure fund to establish the new Iraqi Army.[13] Multi-National Security Transition Command Iraq now had the funds to establish the new army, but Lieutenant General Petraeus needed a larger staff to fix the problem of how to recruit, train, and equip the Iraqi Army. Unfortunately, Lieutenant General Petraeus had a predominately ad-hoc staff, and used existing personnel in theater to fill its manning roster. In spite of this, Petraeus worked through the issues of establishing an army, and focused his efforts toward building an army capable of providing security to the citizens of Iraq. With the mission of the Iraqi Army shifted to counterinsurgency, the U.S. decided to outfit the Iraqi Army with light weapons. Significantly, the U.S. created a table of organization and equipment that was a hybrid between U.S. and old Iraqi Army formations. From that time forward, the fledgling Government of Iraq worked with Multi-National Security Transition Command to augment the Iraqi Army with advanced weapons and equipment. For the time being, the newly created Iraqi Army had to rely on the U.S. for heavy weapons support, artillery support, and aircraft support.

Lieutenant General Petraeus continued to push the U.S. Army, through General Casey, for more personnel. The U.S. Army activated the 98th Division (USAR) from upstate New York to fill his staff and man a new Iraqi Army advisory initiative. Early Iraqi Army failures in Fallujah showed the necessity for an advisory mission to bolster army formations. Although the new advisors partnered with Iraqi Army formations, they were reservists with no training in advising foreign forces. Up to this point, the army had decided that advising foreign forces was a Special Forces mission, but the size of the Iraqi Army re-building effort required the use of conventional military personnel.[14] This first unit of advisors received no specialized advisory training.[15] Furthermore, many of these early advisors failed to embed and live with local Iraqi units, as instructed by Lieutenant General Petraeus. Notably, it is difficult to advise and mentor a counterpart without the willingness to share in the day-to-day struggle.

Lieutenant General Petraeus built a ten-division Iraqi Army through support from Multi-National Force Iraq and coordination with the newly formed Iraqi Government. Nine of the divisions were light infantry equipped with small arms, machine guns, and rocket propelled grenades. One division had Russian built T-72 tanks and BMP infantry fighting vehicles, making it the only heavy weapons division in the Iraqi Army. Additionally, Lieutenant General Petraeus established the framework for institutional training of the Iraqi Army. He established major training centers across Iraq for officer and soldier training, including a state of the art live fire training complex on an old Iraqi tank range east of Baghdad that served as the future main training center for Iraqi battalions and brigades. He staffed these training centers with personnel from Multi-National Security Transition Command Iraq, not advisors embedded with field units. This was significant because advisors and training center personnel fell under different chains of command, adding an unnecessary level of coordination for Iraqi army training. Before Lieutenant General Petraeus handed over command of Multi-National Security Transition Command Iraq to Lieutenant General Martin Dempsey in the summer of 2005, he formed an Iraqi Army of 75,000 personnel through an aggressive recruiting and training program.[16]

Initially, the U.S. Army deployed a Reserve Component division to train and mentor the Iraqi Army. In an effort to foster a large advisory mission aimed at re-building the Iraqi Army, the U.S Army created the Military Transition Team concept in 2005. Military Transition Team's comprised 10 to 15 men, with combat and combat support military occupational specialties. Personnel from across the army, mostly active duty, deployed in support of the advisory mission as part of Military Transition Teams and replaced the 98th Division (USAR) as it rotated home at the completion of its yearlong combat tour. These personnel trained at five different stateside locations for varying amounts of time, with little thought given to standardized advisory training. At least the ad-hoc effort provided an influx of advisors for Iraqi units, albeit with different amounts of advisory competency.[17]

The U.S. Army developed the Military Transition Team concept to mentor and train ten Iraqi army divisions. The following table describes Military Transition Team composition (see table 1). Transition team organization allowed teams to advise Iraqi counterparts in the specialties of maneuver, fires, logistics, communications, and medical support–at least on paper. Advisors focused on trying to institute U.S procedures for an Iraqi Army that lacked the requisite logistical infrastructure or knowledge to fight the same way as the U.S. Army. Keep in mind that advisors had to do this through a significant cultural and language barrier.

Additionally, the U.S. Army struggled throughout the advisory mission to staff Military Transition Teams with personnel who had the correct occupational specialty and experience level required to advise Iraqi Army units because of wartime brigade combat team personnel requirements (see table 1). For example, the U.S. Army commonly staffed fire support and intelligence advisor positions with infantry or armor personnel.[18] This left these soldiers without the requisite experience to advise Iraqi fire support and intelligence officers. It was also commonplace for the U.S. Army to assign personnel for advisory duty without the required rank as outlined in the Military Transition Team concept. Instead, U.S. officers and non-commissioned officers filled positions on Military Transition Teams without the necessary experience to be competent advisors. Furthermore, this rank disparity left advisors mentoring Iraqi counterparts two or three ranks above their own, often leading to questions of legitimacy in the eyes of Iraqi officers.

Table 1. Military Transition Team (MiTT) Composition				
Duty Positions	Career Fields	Battalion MiTT Rank	Brigade MiTT Rank	Division MiTT Rank
Team Chief	Maneuver, Fires, and Effects (MFE)	Major	Lieutenant Colonel	Lieutenant Colonel (Promotable) or Colonel
Staff Maneuver Trainer	MFE	Captain	Major	Lieutenant Colonel
Intelligence Trainer	Operational Support (OS)	Captain	Captain	Captain
Logistics Trainer	Force Sustainment (FS)	Captain	Captain	Captain
Headquarters Support Company Advisor	FS	Captain		
Field Artillery Effects Advisor	MFE	Captain	Captain	Major
Intelligence NCO Trainer	OS	Master Sergeant	Master Sergeant	Master Sergeant
Logistics NCO Trainer	FS	Sergeant First Class	Master Sergeant	Master Sergeant
Field Artillery Effects NCO Advisor	MFE	Sergeant First Class	Sergeant First Class	Master Sergeant
Communications Chief	OS	Sergeant First Class	Staff Sergeant	Staff Sergeant
Medic	Health Services	Specialist - Staff Sergeant	Specialist - Sergeant First Class	Specialist - Sergeant First Class
Signal Company Advisor	OS			Captain
Engineer Company Advisor	MFE			Captain
Ordnance Company Advisor	FS			Captain
Military Police Advisor	MFE			Captain
Military Intelligence Company Advisor	OS			Captain

Source: Mark B. Flynn, Knowledge Management Advisor-Transition Team Forum Facilitator Battle Command Knowledge System (BCKS), OIF MiTT, https://forums.bcks. army.mil/secure/CommunityBrowser.aspx?id=65757&lang=en-US (accessed 4 April 2011).

In an effort to command and control advisory teams across Iraq, Multi-National Corps Iraq established the Provisional Iraq Assistance Group in the summer of 2005, headed by Brigadier General John McLaren (USAR). Multi-National Corps Iraq created this ad-hoc headquarters by using personnel who were already in theater. Furthermore, a convoluted relationship formed between the Iraq Assistance Group and the Military Transition Teams that hindered advisory effectiveness. The Iraq Assistance Group provided administrative control and support to advisory teams but did not control the advisory team's war-fighting mission across Iraq. In effect, this arrangement created two chains of command for the advisory teams. They relied on the Iraq Assistance Group for support, but the brigade combat teams tactically controlled the advisory teams. Meanwhile, Multi-National Security Transition Command Iraq continued to spearhead Iraqi Army training and equipping with no direct command relationship with Military Transition Teams. This added yet another layer of complexity to the advisory mission that often led to confusion and readiness delays for the Iraqi Army.[19]

In the summer of 2005, Multi-National Force Iraq established the Phoenix Academy in Taji, Iraq to improve advisory training and counterinsurgency understanding. The creation of the Phoenix Academy institutionalized advisory training, and allowed advisors to learn and share relevant tactics, techniques, and procedures. Phoenix Academy training provided advisors common training on the functions of advisory duty as well as additional culture and language training. Individuals currently serving as advisors came from across Iraq to the Phoenix Academy to train new advisors, and they shared hard-earned lessons in an effort to train and mentor their Iraqi counterparts. Meanwhile, the U.S. Army created the Counterinsurgency Academy on the same installation as the Phoenix Academy, where U.S. brigade combat leadership discussed counterinsurgency techniques.[20] Each of these academies never synchronized instruction between advisors and brigade combat team leadership. Ultimately, the U.S. Army missed the opportunity to achieve coordination between the advisory mission and brigade combat teams.

The advisory mission began to pay-off, and by June 2006, the Iraqi Army started to take over the control of battle-space from U.S. units. The U.S. Army understood the Military Transition Team concept worked, but the training advisors received needed refinement. In an effort to standardize training for advisors deploying to Iraq, the U.S. Army established the Fort Riley Training Mission. In January 2006, the U.S. Army notified 1st Brigade, 1st Infantry Division to re-structure from a brigade combat team into an advisor-training unit. With the establishment of the Fort Riley Training Mission, all advisors received a standardized sixty-day block of instruction on how to be an advisor. While far from perfect, it was a marked improvement over past efforts with an emphasis on combat proficiency and introduction to language and culture. Soldiers received twenty hours of language training and multiple blocks of instruction on culture. This did not create fluent Arabic speakers, but at least it exposed advisors to their future environment. An added benefit of centralized training was that teams formed stateside, and thus had two months to build relationships with each other prior to deployment.[21] Interestingly, many of the advisory trainers never served as advisors, which led to advisor frustration over the program of instruction.

In addition to the creation of the Fort Riley Training Mission, the U.S. Army notified the 1st Infantry Division to staff the Iraq Assistance Group. In June 2006, the 1st Infantry Division provided an assistant division commander, Brigadier General Dana Pittard, to lead the Iraq Assistance Group, and used joint personnel from all services to staff the headquarters. With the 1st Infantry Division in control of the Iraq Assistance

Group, coordination with the Fort Riley Training Mission dramatically increased. The Iraq Assistance Group maintained administrative support of advisors in Iraq and instituted initiatives such as pre-deployment site surveys and video teleconferences for advisors. This increased situational awareness for advisor teams, and allowed the transfer of knowledge amongst teams in training and advisors in combat. The Iraq Assistance group maintained oversight of all efforts improving training coordination between stateside trainers and the Phoenix Academy. In the end, the Iraq Assistance Group created a more complete advisor by ensuring that each stage of advisory training emphasized advisory tactics, techniques, and procedures used in Iraq.[22]

Moreover, an important milestone occurred on 3 May 2006, with the establishment of the Iraqi Ground Forces Command. The new command served as the future operational headquarters of all Iraqi Army units, co-located with the U.S. headquarters in Camp Victory, Iraq. Over time, the Iraqi Ground Forces Command took operational ownership of Iraqi Army units and employed them in support of the Government of Iraq. The Iraq Assistance Group focused heavily on advising the Iraqi Ground Forces Command to speed the process of turning over operational control of Iraqi Army units.

Throughout 2006 and 2007, the Iraqi Army continued to grow, many times without the U.S. knowing about it. What were once ten Iraqi Army divisions grew to thirteen Iraqi Army divisions, and they all required advisors to partner with and mentor them. Interestingly, as the Government of Iraq created additional units, Multi-National Force Iraq insisted on supporting new units with advisors, thus creating an advisory coverage problem for the U.S. Army. Originally, the U.S. Army created the Military

Transition Team concept to advise a ten division Iraqi Army, requiring Multi-National Corps Iraq to use creative solutions to cover a thirteen division Iraqi Army with advisory support. This required many transition teams to advise multiple Iraqi Army units. Additionally, brigade combat teams created additional transition teams using personnel from their respective brigade. In addition to the advisory mission, Multi-National Security Transition Command had to scramble to outfit the new divisions with equipment.

In early 2007, General Petraeus took command of Multi-National Force Iraq, and implemented a new counterinsurgency strategy across Iraq that required U.S. soldiers to live amongst the Iraqi people. His efforts required U.S. and Iraqi units to work together to bring security to the population. This counterinsurgency operation required coordination between Iraqi Army, Iraqi Police, and U.S. Army units to secure Baghdad. Furthermore, this new counterinsurgency effort required Military Transition Teams to live with their Iraqi Counterparts amongst the population in small combat outposts, commonly referred to as Joint Security Stations. Prior to the establishment of small combat outposts, many advisors did not live with their Iraqi counterparts. Conversely, the new counterinsurgency strategy embedded advisors in Iraqi units at all times, and the Iraqi Army units flourished.

At the height of the Military Transition Team advisory mission, there were two hundred fifty advisor teams totaling approximately 3,000 personnel embedded with Iraqi Army units.[23] The Military Transition Team concept required ten brigade combat teams worth of U.S. Army officers and non-commissioned officers to serve as advisors. The U.S. Army could not expand transition teams because the personnel to fill advisory teams had to fill brigade combat teams deploying to combat in Iraq and Afghanistan. In April

2007, Multi-National Corps Iraq gave brigade combat teams operational control of Military Transition Teams. Many commanders, seeing the Iraqi Army as vital to mission success, augmented existing transition teams with extra personnel and created additional teams with brigade combat team personnel to advise the growing Iraqi Army.[24] Assigning advisors directly to brigade combat teams allowed Multi-National Force Iraq to increase the advisory mission to the expanded Iraqi Army.

On 3 July 2008, in an effort to show the U.S. Army's dedication to the advisory mission, the Chief of Staff of the U.S. Army, General Casey, announced that service on an advisory team counted as key developmental time for field grade officers. Field grade officers require twelve months of key developmental time for promotion to the next rank, and General Casey's decision elevated advisory experience as equivalent to basic branch field grade officer key developmental experience. Additionally, General Casey gave the promotion board guidance to look favorably on Military Transition Team experience. Significantly, he also mandated selection of Military Transition Team leaders from the Centralized Selection List, traditionally used to select battalion commanders. In effect, General Casey made Military Transition Team leader service equivalent to traditional battalion command.[25]

By 2009, the Iraqi Army demonstrated expanded capability while conducting counterinsurgency operations across Iraq. In conjunction with its advisors, the Iraqi Army defeated insurgencies in Basra, Baghdad, Al-Anbar Province, and Baquba. The security situation improved throughout Iraq, with U.S. and Iraqi casualties falling to levels not seen since 2004.[26] As of 1 January 2009, the Iraqi Army owned responsibility for all security efforts in Iraq with the U.S. Army in a supporting role per agreements made between the Iraqi and U.S. government. Additionally, by September 2009, the U.S. Army stopped training and deploying Military Transition Teams to advise the Iraqi Army. Instead, the U.S. Army designated certain brigade combat teams deploying to Iraq as Advise and Assist Brigades. Instead of building hundreds of 10 to 15 man Military Transition Teams, the U.S. Army augmented traditional brigade combat teams with forty-eight additional field grade officers. These advisors coupled with additional brigade combat team personnel serving in a support of the advisory mission, advised the Iraqi Army. In effect, the new Advise and Assist Brigade concept cut advisory personnel requirements in half compared to Military Transition Teams. Altogether, the Advise and Assist Brigade concept placed the onus of advising Iraqi Army units on the brigade combat team.[27] Implementation of the new security agreement between the Government of Iraq and the United States ensured U.S. forces focused on promotion and encouragement of host-nation efforts.[28] Additionally, Multi-National Force Iraq de-activated the Iraq Assistance Group because Military Transition Teams no longer existed. Iraq Assistance Group's administrative support to advisors was no longer necessary because support to advisory missions came from the brigade combat team.

Meanwhile, in September 2009, U.S. Army advisory training moved from Fort Riley, Kansas to Fort Polk, Louisiana, and the Phoenix Academy closed its doors in Taji, Iraq. The U.S Army established the 162nd Infantry Training Brigade at Fort Polk to train the advisory mission, further cementing the U.S. Army's commitment to train advisors in Iraq as well as future conflicts. The 162nd Infantry Training Brigade no longer trained advisors at a consolidated location; instead, it took the training to stateside brigade combat team locations prior to the brigade combat team's deployment. The 162nd

74

Infantry Training Brigade focuses on training the whole brigade for advisory operations and not just the forty-eight augmented advisors in the brigade.[29] Additionally, designated Advise and Assist Brigade advisors conduct a two-week advisory focused program of instruction known as the Advisor Academy at Fort Polk, Louisiana or the unit's home station prior to deployment. While similar to the advisor training conducted at Fort Riley, advisors do not focus on combat tasks. Instead, this training focuses completely on counterinsurgency, culture, language, and key leader engagement training, with established metrics to evaluate advisor performance. For example, in coordination with the Defense Language institute advisors receive eighteen hours of language training that culminates with a language examination. This exam requires advisors to show proficiency in fifty to seventy Arabic phrases. This training does not create language or cultural experts, but exposes advisors to host-nation languages and culture. Furthermore, the Defense Language Institute works with advisors to increase language proficiency through self-paced online instruction after completion of the Advisor Academy.

After closing the Phoenix Academy in Taji, the U.S. Army opened the Stability Center of Excellence in Camp Victory, Iraq to focus U.S. military leadership on its new role in Iraq.[30] On 19 August 2010, the U.S. Army re-deployed the last combat brigade from Iraq. All brigade combat teams serving in Iraq advise Iraqi Security Forces using the Advise and Assist Brigade concept.[31] These seven brigade combat teams function as Advise and Assist Brigades, with advisors serving at the Iraqi brigade level and above. These advisor brigades comprise the majority of the 50,000 personnel operating in Iraq.[32] With the reduction of personnel, the U.S. Army re-flagged Multi-National Force Iraq to U.S. Forces Iraq because of the smaller mission in Iraq.

During the last eight years, the U.S. Army built an Iraqi Army comprising seventeen-divisions and over 220,000 personnel with the capacity and capability to provide security to the population, and support the Iraqi government. Ultimately, the Iraqi Government wants to establish a twenty-division army. Current advisory missions now focus on building an Iraqi Army capable of thwarting external threats. Recently, the Iraqi Army with U.S. support is fielding advanced weapons systems such as the M-1 tank, M-16 rifle, armored infantry vehicles, mortar systems, and artillery systems.[33] The final step in the U.S. advisory mission is to ensure that Iraq can defend itself from external threats when U.S. military forces withdraw in December 2011.[34]

South Korean Advisory Mission and Iraqi Advisory Mission Comparison

From 1946 to 1953 the U.S. Army conducted its first large scale security force assistance effort to build and train the R.O.K. Army to defeat the Communist NKPA.[35] Fifty years after the armistice with North Korea, the U.S. Army conducted combat operations against the Baathist Regime of Iraq, resulting in the destruction of the Iraqi Army. U.S. Army leadership failed to predict the future advisory mission to rebuild the Iraqi Army.[36] While the efforts to train a R.O.K. Army began prior to hostilities with North Korea, the effort to train an Iraqi Army began after the defeat of Saddam Hussein's Baath Party Regime.

Each war brought with it political baggage that threatened the American effort to train an effective host-nation army. In Korea, U.S. fiscal responsibility and hesitancy to build a R.O.K. national defense force for fears of sparking conflict with the Soviet Union drove policy makers to limit the size and capability of the R.O.K. Army prior to conflict

76

with North Korea.[37] Once war began on 25 June 1950, the R.O.K. Army was unprepared and unable to defend R.O.K. territory from the NKPA assault. With the R.O.K. Army defeated and scattered, KMAG had to re-build the R.O.K. Army to defend South Korea.[38] Similarly, in Iraq, political and military policy muddied efforts to build an Iraqi Army. Post invasion military planners failed to predict the insurgency in late 2003 that ripped the country apart through sectarian violence for the next eight years. Additionally, U.S. civilian leadership dissolved the Saddam Era Iraqi Army without coordination with U.S. military leadership.[39] This decision meant that organizing an Iraqi Army had to start from scratch. In both South Korea and Iraq, U.S. policy makers and military leaders failed to coordinate efforts to organize and train the host-nation army.

The establishment of KMAG on 29 April 1949 marked America's commitment to establish a permanent advisory mission to train the R.O.K. Army.[40] Similarly, the establishment of Military Transition Teams in Iraq in the summer of 2005 marked the beginning of American advisory commitment to the Iraqi Army.[41] Each advisory mission faced challenges to establish an effective host nation army.

In South Korea, KMAG created a lightly equipped counterinsurgency force following U.S. occupation of South Korea after 1945. U.S. policy mandated that the R.O.K. Army be equipped only with light weapons. Prior to the invasion of South Korea, KMAG trained and equipped a 100,000 man R.O.K. Army to assist with internal security. By 1949, American policy changed to equip and train the R.O.K.A. to defend South Korea from external attacks.[42] However, KMAG did not have the time or equipment to train the R.O.K. Army for major combat operations. After the invasion of South Korea, KMAG's previous training experience expedited the re-establishment of R.O.K.A.

training systems.[43] In a span of only three years, the R.O.K. Army grew from 22,000 personnel to an army of twenty-divisions and 576,000 personnel. Finally, U.S. policy equipped the R.O.K. Army with the necessary heavy weapons to conduct major combat operations.[44]

At its peak, KMAG employed 2,866 personnel to train an army of 576,000 personnel. These advisors typically operated in two to six man teams, and embedded at the battalion, regiment, division, and training school level.[45] Notably, most advisory emphasis was at the regimental level, as this was the common tactical organization in the Korean War. Throughout the conflict, the U.S. Army's Reserve Component bore the brunt of advisory duty, with 81 percent of advisors coming from the reserve ranks.[46]

The advisory mission in Iraq built an Iraqi Army with different objectives than the advisory mission in South Korea. The U.S. Army destroyed the conventional Iraqi Army, and struggled to build a capable counterinsurgency force following combat operations in March 2003. However, in South Korea KMAG needed to transform a counterinsurgency force into a force capable of defeating a conventional threat. All U.S. efforts to recruit, train, and equip an Iraqi Army were created from scratch with the abolishment of the old Iraqi Army.[47] The training of a new Iraqi Army started when Multi-National Security Transition Command Iraq, upon its establishment in June 2004, began working with the fledgling Iraqi Government to equip and train a ten division lightly equipped counterinsurgency focused Iraqi Army.[48] The U.S. Army established 10 to 15 man Military Transition Teams to train and mentor the Iraqi Army much in the same way KMAG advisors worked with R.O.K. Army counterparts. As compared to KMAG, the U.S. advisory mission was not all-inclusive. KMAG trained, equipped, and advised the

R.O.K. Army whereas the U.S. advisory mission in Iraq developed multiple commands responsible for the different functions of training, equipping, and advising the Iraqi Army.

From 2005 to -2009 Military Transition Teams comprised the bulk of the advisory mission, and comprised 250 teams and over 3,000 advisory personnel. These personnel advised Iraqi units at the battalion, brigade, division, command operations centers, and Iraqi Ground Forces Command level to prepare them to take the lead in counterinsurgency operations across Iraq. Unlike in Korea, the U.S. Army developed a metric to evaluate Iraqi Army units, known as the Operational Readiness Assessment. Military transition teams conducted a monthly assessment on their Iraqi Army unit's capabilities, and rated them on a scale of one to four. If a unit reached Operational Readiness Assessment level two, they no longer required advisor support. This assessment was subjective and relied on Military Transition Team leaders' opinions on the effectiveness of their Iraqi Army unit. Teams often used the assessment tool as a methodology to make the team look as if it was accomplishing its mission. Prior to re-deployment, it was common practice for advisors assess to give a unit higher ratings in order to show progress during their tenure. Additionally, new advisor teams rated units poorly to leave room for improvement during their tour. Even with the problems of the assessment, Multi-National Corps Iraq used this system to take advisors away from Iraqi Army units that reached an assessment level of two or less. Multi-National Corps Iraq planners used this flawed system to re-assign Military Transition Teams to newly generated Iraqi Army units, leaving inaccurately assessed Iraqi units without access to combat enablers that advisors provided. Throughout the advisory mission in Iraq, military planners at Multi-National Corps Iraq, and later U.S. Forces Iraq, used the Operational

Readiness Assessment to stop advising units at the battalion level and focus advisory

missions at the brigade level and higher because of the limited number of Military

Transition Teams.[49] However, in South Korea KMAG maintained coverage of all R.O.K.

Army units as it conducted major combat operations because embedded advisors

provided vital links to U.S. units sharing the same defensive perimeter as R.O.K. Army

units.

In September 2009, the U.S. Army abandoned the Military Transition Team

concept and designated certain brigade combat teams as Advise and Assist Brigades.

Multi-National Corps Iraq implemented a brigade centric advisory concept that was

unlike anything used by KMAG. In South Korea, U.S. Army units relied heavily on

R.O.K. Army units for offensive and defensive operations against the NKPA that fostered

a close relationship between KMAG advisors and U.S. Army units. U.S. Army units in

Iraq never achieved the same level of synchronization with Military Transition Team

advisors that KMAG experienced in South Korea. Besides the obvious ease of pressure

on the U.S. Army personnel system, the Advise and Assist Brigade concept allowed

brigade commanders to synchronize all aspects of the advisory mission in Iraq because

their sole mission was to enable the effectiveness of the Iraqi Army.

South Korean and Iraqi Cultural and Ethnic Paradigms

In both South Korea and Iraq, advisors struggled with cultural and ethnic

paradigms that threatened mission success. Throughout the South Korean advisory

mission, political necessity required the U.S. administration to sever colonial Japanese

influence, but R.O.K. Army leaders had Japanese military training.[50] Without advisory assistance, R.O.K. Army soldiers reverted to suicidal banzai Japanese tactics taught prior to the U.S. occupation.[51] Through necessity, KMAG worked with R.O.K. Army officers to extinguish Japanese influence and through a thorough retraining program built a capable R.O.K. Army that no longer mirrored the Japanese Colonial Army.

In addition to Japanese influence, a communist insurgency motivated by North Korea threatened national security. In 1948, communist infiltrators in the Constabulary mutinied and otherwise threatened security inside of South Korea.[52] KMAG's predecessor, PMAG, worked with the Constabulary to identify communist elements and remove them from the ranks, while also implementing screening efforts to reduce communist infiltration of the organization.[53] These screening efforts carried forward in the new R.O.K. Army. Fortunately, South Koreans displayed intense nationalistic pride that aided KMAG efforts to deny Japanese and communist influence inside the R.O.K. Army.

Throughout the conflict in Iraq, U.S. Army leadership faced the problem of sectarian strife. In many ways, Iraq did not represent a nation; it represented three independent groups vying for power.[54] The minority Sunni Muslim population yearned to re-establish the power it lost with the destruction of the Baathist Regime, the majority Shiite Muslim population wanted to assert itself as the new face of power in Iraq, and the Kurds occupying Northern Iraq wanted an autonomous nation-state.[55] The one institution in Iraqi history that represented all of the Iraqi people was the Iraqi Army, dissolved in May 2003.[56] A heavy burden lay on the advisory mission in Iraq to re-build the Iraqi Army amidst the sectarian strife. Only the development of an Iraqi Army that represented all of Iraq could bring order to the country.[57] Early on, Iraqi Army units refused to operate amongst the population for fear of retribution or because they supported the insurgency. Sectarian strife turned into outright civil war on 22 February 2006 with the bombing of the Shiite Al-Askari Mosque Samarra by Sunni extremists.[58] To quell the violence the U.S. military and advisors worked with the Iraqi Army to defeat the insurgency through a new population-centric counterinsurgency strategy implemented by General Petraeus.[59] Through patience and diligence, the U.S. advisory mission empowered Iraqi leadership, trained capable units, and outfitted them properly to defeat the insurgency. Over time, and despite several challenges, the advisory mission helped the Iraqi's build an army capable of protecting the interests of all Iraqis.

Each advisory mission dealt with dynamic social, cultural, and ethnic challenges, from erasing the effects of Japanese colonialism to advising a primarily Shiite Iraqi Army unit in a Sunni neighborhood. In many ways, these challenges define the problem of any advisory mission. In addition to these challenges, advisors in both conflicts lacked the ability to communicate with their host nation counterparts, which added a layer of complexity to the challenges advisors faced. Each advisory mission relied heavily on interpreters to build relationships with counterparts and conduct the training and mentoring of the host-nation army.[60]

Regardless of the conflict, advisors train forces on organizational development, doctrine, logistics, and tactical employment of weapons systems, but the human dimension provides the uniqueness that defines individual advisory missions. The combination of cultures and languages involved in advisory missions change from one conflict to the next. Advisory success may come down to personnel who can immerse themselves in foreign cultures, and learn the local language. In South Korea, Captain

James Hausman positively affected the fledgling advisory mission because he had an interest in the culture and an ability to relate to his counterparts. KMAG after action reviews emphasize interest in foreign cultures as a prerequisite for advisory selection. In Iraq, the U.S. Army recognized cultural and language training as the foundation of advisory preparation, but failed to provide training about cultural differences at anything above a superficial level because of time constraints. Understanding the nature of the conflict, and educating soldiers so that they can embrace and gain familiarity with foreign cultures may prove beneficial to establishing future advisory missions.

KMAG and Iraqi Advisory Training and Operations Comparison

The initial advisory mission in Iraq relied on a Reserve Component division for advisors to the Iraqi Army, but later efforts employed predominantly active component advisors through Military Transition Teams and the Advise and Assist Brigade concept. In the Korean War, Reserve Component personnel dominated the advisory mission. In both advisory missions soldiers with the appropriate occupational specialty, a need for combat experience, and the required rank found themselves in advisory duty.[61] Interestingly, personnel specialists in the U.S. Army used no metric to fill combat advisor positions, despite the fact that U.S. Army doctrine explains that not everyone can be a combat advisor due to the complexity of the mission.[62] Notably, each advisory mission required soldiers to advise counterparts at a rank above their own, sometimes leading to questions of legitimacy by their host-nation counterparts. This is because the U.S. Army staffed the advisory missions with soldiers of lesser rank than their counterparts. In each case, the U.S. Army developed ambitious advisory staffing requirements, while also attempting to staff units for combat. When all staffing requirements are a priority, none of them is a priority.

In both conflicts, the U.S. Army organized an advisory mission in very different ways but achieved similar results. In the end, the result was the formation of a national army. KMAG advisors received no additional training to conduct advisory duty with the R.O.K. Army other than their basic branch specific training. Upon assignment, advisors reported to KMAG for a series of in-briefings to familiarize the advisor with their next assignment. At the end of the in-briefings, KMAG handed each advisor a handbook that described the various job details of advisory duty.[63] Interestingly, KMAG advisory missions proved successful even without additional preparatory advisory training. Multiple reasons exist for this success: the R.O.K. Army command relationship with USAFIK, an effort by advisors to share relevant tactics, techniques, and procedures amongst advisors, and the fact that KMAG owned all facets of the advisory mission.

In Iraq, the advisory mission began in an ad-hoc fashion similar to KMAG, but grew into a coordinated training effort. Unlike in KMAG, however, Military Transition Teams bound for Iraq organized as a 10 to 15 man team and conducted two months of combat focused advisory training.[64] Though far from perfect, at least Iraq advisors received advisory training prior to deployment. KMAG training consisted of a country in brief with no emphasis on language or cultural training. In the new Advise and Assist Brigade, the U.S. Army assigns advisors to the brigade combat team prior to deployment, allowing advisors to form relationships with the brigade that will support them in combat.[65] Significantly, the U.S. Army established the 162nd Infantry Training Brigade, under Training and Doctrine Command, to focus on advisor training and capture advisory lessons learned. The U.S. Army should maintain the 162nd Advisor Training Brigade to train advisors for future conflicts and institutionalize Security Force Assistance education to avoid repeating similar mistakes.

If a KMAG advisor experienced an issue he contacted KMAG for a solution, whereas in Iraq advisors needed to coordinate with multiple agencies. Additionally, the streamlined command relationship between the R.O.K. Army and USAFIK meant that USAFIK owned all R.O.K. Army units and their emplacement on the battlefield. U.S. Army units relied heavily on the R.O.K. Army in battle against communist forces. However, the Government of Iraq maintained control of Iraqi forces, and many times the U.S. Army found itself in a reactionary mode to cover newly created Iraqi forces with advisors, and access to combat enablers such as artillery and aircraft support.

The advisory missions in Korea and Iraq show similarity through the effort to share relevant tactics, techniques, and procedures amongst advisors. While KMAG relied primarily on the KMAG Handbook, the Iraq advisory mission had the benefit of the communications age to increase information dissemination.[66] Advisors shared knowledge across the U.S. Army in professional publications, internet based knowledge sharing networks, blogs, and doctrine writing such as the counterinsurgency field manual. Significantly, advisors to the Iraqi Army, unlike in Korea, experienced near real-time access to relevant tactics, techniques, and procedures for advisory operations. The U.S. Army has advisory experience spanning over a century, but continues to re-learn hard fought lessons in each new advisory mission. The challenge for the U.S. Army is to capture this experience for future advisory mission training.

85

KMAG and Iraq Advisor Qualities

After the Korean War, the Human Resources Research Organization, a subsidiary of the Research and Development Department of the Army, and the Operations Research Office at John Hopkins University, conducted surveys of KMAG advisors to identify characteristics of advisors for future advisory missions. Over 80 percent of KMAG advisors described patience and tact as essential traits of advisors.[67] Additionally, the ability to build rapport and establish a cordial relationship with host-nation counterparts affected advisory success. KMAG policy during the Korean War was to reassign advisors if they did not get along with their counterparts.[68] Notably, R.O.K. Army counterparts considered the lack of a cordial personality more important than technical competence in their American counterparts.[69] These studies highlight that an advisor must work past the language barrier to achieve mutual understanding with their counterpart.[70] Additionally, many R.O.K. Army officers complained that American advisors were rude and lacked empathy for the Korean culture.[71] As for job experience, KMAG officers recommended assigning officers for advisory duty with combat experience in order to give advisors legitimacy in front of R.O.K. Army officers with as much as three years of combat experience. The survey of KMAG advisors pointed out that the R.O.K. Army formation is only as good as the KMAG officer assigned to it. Many KMAG advisors viewed U.S. Army command experience as more useful to advisory duty than institutional training expertise.[72]

As with KMAG, the U.S. Army has studied the Iraq Advisory mission to identify characteristics of advisors for future advisory missions. In 2008, the U.S. Army Research Institute in cooperation with the Joint Center for International Security Force Assistance conducted a study on the characteristics of advisors in the Middle East. This research recognized tactical and technical proficiency as paramount to success with host-nation counterparts. Furthermore, this study highlights tact, positive attitude, and empathy toward a foreign culture as necessary traits for advisors.[73] Additionally, the Joint Center for International Security Force Assistance published a *Security Force Assistance Handbook for Commanders* that describes patience, perseverance, and empathy as essential traits of soldiers selected for advisory duty. In addition to these characteristics, advisors serve as the role model for their counterpart and should act in ways commensurate with this duty.[74]

Studies of KMAG and Iraqi advisor traits highlight similar characteristics even though the operations span fifty years of military experience. Current doctrine acknowledges that not everyone can serve as an advisor, but in both the Korean and Iraq War, no one has implemented a solution to assign personnel that exhibit these traits.[75] The current mantra of the U.S. Army is full-spectrum operations, whereby soldiers must be proficient at all tasks, including Security Force Assistance.[76] The U.S. Army is rushing to failure if it believes that it can mold any soldier into an advisor. The South Korean and Iraq advisory missions demonstrate the importance of advisor selection through measurable traits, and unless the U.S. Army codifies an advisor selection system to choose the most capable personnel it will hamper future Security Force Assistance missions.

[1]—President Bush addresses the Nation," *Washington Post*, 20 September 2001, http://www.washingtonpost.com/wpsrv/nation/specials/attacked/transcripts/bushaddress_092001.html (accessed 21 November 2010).

[2]Yossef Bodansky, *The Secret History of the Iraq War* (New York: HarperCollins Publishers, 2004), 272.

[3]David Cloud and Greg Jaffe, *The Fourth Star* (New York: Crown Publishers, 2009), 118.

[4]Ibid., 123.

[5]Donald Wright and Timothy Reese, *On Point II* (Fort Leavenworth, KS: Combat Studies Institute Press, 2008), 30.

[6]Cloud and Jaffe, *The Fourth Star*, 128; Wright and Reese, *On Point II*, 32.

[7]Rajiv Chandrasekaran, "U.S. to Form New Iraqi Army," *The Washington Post*, 24 June 2003, www.iraqwararchive.org/data/jun24/US/wp06.pdf (accessed 14 March 2011).

[8]Dahr Jamail, "No End in Sight as Fallujah Death Toll Approaches 700," *The New Standard*, 11 April 2004, http://newstandardnews.net/content/index.cfm/items/169 (accessed 14 March 2011).

[9]Aaron Boal, "On the Ground: Training Indigenous Forces in Iraq," in *Turning Victory into Success*, ed. Brian De Toy (Fort Leavenworth, KS: Combat Studies Institute Press, 2004), 287.

[10]Ibid., 288-289.

[11]Anthony Cordesman and Patrick Baetjer, *Iraqi Security Forces: A Strategy for Success* (Westport, CT: Praeger Security International, 2006), 147-148.

[12]Cloud and Jaffe, *The Fourth Star*, 170.

[13] Ibid., 175.

[14]Ibid., 178-179.

[15]LTC Curtis Hudson, Commander 4th BN, 353rd Infantry Regiment, 162nd Infantry Training Brigade, Interview by author, 8 January 2011.

[16]Cloud and Jaffe, *The Fourth Star*, 210.

[17]Hudson, Interview.

[18]LTC David Wood, Commander 1st BN, 353rd Infantry Regiment, 162nd Infantry Training Brigade, Interview by author, 8 January 2011.

[19]Hudson, Interview.

[20]Cloud and Jaffe, *The Fourth Star*, 204.

[21]Hudson, Interview.

[22]Ibid.

[23]Wood, Interview.

[24]Hudson, Interview.

[25]Todd Lopez, ―Transition Team makes Officers Competitive for Promotion,‖ *Army.Mil News,* 3 July 2008, http://www.army.mil/-news/2008/07/03/10613-transition-team-experience-makes-officers-competitive-for-promotion/ (accessed 20 January 2011).

[26]Cloud and Jaffe, *The Fourth Star*, 204.

[27]Wood, Interview.

[28]Colonel Phillip Battaglia and Lieutenant Colonel Curtis Taylor, ―Security Force Assistance Operations: Defining the Advise and Assist Brigade,‖ *Military Review* (July-August 2010): 2.

[29]Wood, Interview.

[30]Ibid.

[31]Richard Engel and Charlene Gubash, ―Lasfull U.S. Combat Brigade Leaves Iraq,‖ *MSNBC,* 19 August 2010, http://www.msnbc.msn.com/id/38744453/ns/world_news-mideast/n_africa/ (accessed 14 March 2011).

[32]Wood, Interview.

[33]Global Security, ―The Iraqi Army,‖ http://www.globalsecurity.org/military/world/iraq/nia.htm (accessed 14 March 2011); Wood, Interview.

[34]―Obama: U.S. to Withdraw Most Iraq Troops by August 2010,‖ *CNN,* 29 February 2009, http://articles.cnn.com/2009-02-27/politics/obama.troops_1_iraq-troops-home president-obama?_s=PM:POLITICS (accessed 14 March 2011).

[35]Sheila Jager, ―Iraqi Security Forces and Lessons from Korea,‖ *Strategic Studies Institute Editorial* (December 2006), 2-1.

[36]Fontenot, Degen, and Tohn, *On Point*, 29.

[37]Peter Clemens, ―Captain James Hausman, U.S. Army Military Advisor to Korea, 1946-48: The Intelligent Man on the Spot,‖ *Journal of Strategic Studies* 25, no. 1 (March 2002): 169.

[38]Robert Sawyer, *Military Advisors in Korea: KMAG in Peace and War* (Washington, DC: Office of the Chief of Military History, 1962), 146.

[39]Coalition Provision Authority Order # 2, http://www.iraqcoalition.org/ regulations/20030823_CPAORD_2_Dissolution_of_Entities_with_Annex_A.pdf (accessed 14 March 2011).

[40]Sawyer, *Military Advisors in Korea*, 45.

[41]Hudson, Interview.

[42]Gregg Brazinsky, *Nation Building in South Korea* (Chapel Hill: University of North Carolina Press, 2007), 78.

[43]Sawyer, *Military Advisors in Korea*, 150-151.

[44]Robert Ramsey, *Advising Indigenous Forces: American Advisors in Korea, Vietnam, and El Salvador* (Fort Leavenworth, KS: Combat Studies Institute Press, 2006), 10.

[45]Sawyer, *Military Advisors in Korea*, 162-163.

[46]Alfred Hausrath, *The KMAG Advisor: Role and Problems of the Military Advisor in Developing an Indigenous Army for Combat Operations in Korea* (Chevy Chase, MD: Operational Research Office, Johns Hopkins University, 1957), 109.

[47]Coalition Provision Authority Order # 2, http://www.iraqcoalition.org/ regulations/20030823_CPAORD_2_Dissolution_of_Entities_with_Annex_A.pdf (accessed 14 March 2011).

[48]Cloud and Jaffe, *The Fourth Star*, 170.

[49]Hudson, Interview.

[50]Clemens, ―Captain James Hausman," 176; Allan Millett, *The War For Korea: 1945-1950: A House Burning* (Lawrence, KS: University Press of Kansas, 2005), 105.

[51]Sawyer, *Military Advisors in Korea*, 25.

[52]Korean Institute of Military History, *The Korean War*, Vol. I (Lincoln, NE: University of Nebraska Press 2000-2001), 27-28.

[53]Sawyer, *Military Advisors in Korea*, 39-40.

[54]Bodansky, *The Secret History of the Iraq*, 368.

[55]Cloud and Jaffe, *The Fourth Star*, 139.

[56]Coalition Provision Authority Order # 2, http://www.iraqcoalition.org/regulations/20030823_CPAORD_2_Dissolution_of_Entities_with_Annex_A.pdf (accessed 14 March 2011).

[57]Cloud and Jaffe, *The Fourth Star*, 170.

[58]Ibid., 224.

[59]Ibid., 274-275.

[60]Alfred Hausrath, *The KMAG Advisor*, 67-68; Captain Jared Kite, Major Christopher Matson, and Lieutenant Colonel Richard McConnell, ―So You're Going to be on a MiTT," *Field Artillery* (November-December 2006): 41.

[61]Ramsey, *Advising Indigenous Forces*, 11.

[62]U.S. Army, Field Manual 3-07.1, *Security Force Assistance* (Washington, DC: Government Printing Office, 2009), 7-3; Hudson, Interview; Wood, Interview.

[63]Sawyer, *Military Advisors in Korea*, 57.

[64]Hudson, Interview.

[65]Wood, Interview.

[66]Sawyer, *Military Advisors in Korea*, 44-45.

[67]Hausrath, *The KMAG Advisor*, 28.

[68]Dean Froehlich, *Military Advisors and Counterparts in Korea: A Study of Personal Traits and Characteristics* (Washington, DC: Research and Development Department of the Army, 1970), 3.

[69]Hausrath, *The KMAG Advisor*, 28-29.

[70]Froehlich, *Military Advisors and Counterparts in Korea*, 3.

[71]Hausrath, *The KMAG Advisor*, 30.

[72]Ibid., 25-26.

[73]Michelle Zbylut, Kimberly Metcalf, Brandon McGowen, Michael Beemer, Christopher Vowels, and Jason Brunner, *Raw Comments from Cross-Cultural Survey* attachment in *An Analysis of Cross-Cultural Behaviors for Military Advisors in the Middle East* (Fort Leavenworth, KS: U.S. Army Research Institute for the Behavioral and Social Sciences and Joint Center for Security Force Assistance, 2008), 1.

[74]Joint Center for International Security Force Assistance. *Commander's Handbook for Security Force Assistance* (Fort Leavenworth, KS: JCISFA, 2008), 5.

[75]U.S. Army, Field Manual 3-07.1, *Security Force Assistance*, 7-3; Hudson, Interview; Wood, Interview.

[76]U.S. Army, Field Manual 7-0, *Training for Full Spectrum Operations* (Washington, DC: Government Printing Office, 2008), 1-7.

CHAPTER 5

CONCLUSIONS

> Not every Soldier is well suited to perform advisory functions; even those considered to be the best and most experienced have failed at being an advisor. Effective advisors are only the most capable individuals. Advisors are Soldiers known to take the initiative and who set the standards for others; however, they are also patient and personable enough to work effectively with FSF. Recognizing that not all Soldiers are capable of performing as advisors, leaders should immediately remove advisors who do not exhibit these qualities.
> —U.S. Army, Field Manual 3-07.1, *Security Force Assistance*

After the invasion of South Korea by the NKPA on 25 June 1950, the R.O.K. Army lay dispersed across South Korea.[1] Embedded KMAG advisors salvaged remnants of the R.O.K. Army and conducted a fighting withdrawal to the south. In conjunction with U.S. forces, the R.O.K. Army valiantly defended and repelled the NKPA over the next four years. From 1950 to 1953, KMAG worked with R.O.K.A. leadership to train and equip a twenty-division army, ultimately organizing an army of 576,000 personnel capable of modern combined arms warfare.[2]

By 1953, the fighting in Korea reached a stalemate at the 38th Parallel between the communist supported NKPA and the U.S. led United Nations forces. Cease-fire negotiations began, but the fighting continued.[3] In a last ditch effort to improve North Korea's bargaining power, communist forces launched a massive attack along R.O.K. Army defensive positions in Kumsong.[4] If the R.O.K. Army failed to block the offensive, fighting would have continued. However, R.O.K.A success at Kumsong could provide the advantage to negotiate a cease-fire. Although the R.O.K. Army lost ground to the communist forces, it did not break. After enduring heavy losses, the R.O.K. Army reformed and launched local counterattacks, preventing enemy penetration deep into the Eighth Army's defensive perimeter.[5]

The R.O.K. Army reform, instituted and orchestrated by KMAG, was a success principally because of General Van Fleet's focus on R.O.K. Army leadership.[6] For instance, during the July 1953 communist offensive, R.O.K. Army leaders maintained their defensive perimeter and mounted counterattacks, demonstrating newfound resolve and competency. Just two years earlier, R.O.K. Army units failed to repel NKPA assaults and retreated. From 1950 to 1953, KMAG advisors, though small in numbers, worked feverishly with counterparts to build rapport and provide them with the necessary tools to accomplish the mission. In the end, the performance of the R.O.K. Army ensured a cease-fire between North and South Korea on 27 July 1953.[7]

The United States of America finds itself involved in another large-scale advisory mission in Iraq, fifty years after the Korean War. The advisory mission in Iraq shows that the U.S. Army failed to grasp and codify lessons learned from the South Korean advisory mission. In each case the U.S. Army recruited, trained, and equipped massive national armies with largely ad-hoc advisory organizations. The biggest lesson-learned from an organizational standpoint in Korea was the effectiveness of creating an advisor organization responsible for all facets of building the South Korean Army. The U.S. Army failed to grasp this when entering Iraq, and created a convoluted command and control structure that stumps even the smartest people. In Iraq, advisors had to coordinate with multiple agencies for recruiting, equipping, training, and advising the Iraqi Army. However, KMAG had the flexibility to solve problems in-house because of a unified advisory command and control structure. All future advisory missions should achieve unity of effort by recruiting, equipping, training, and advising foreign forces under one chain of command.

Moreover, the advisory missions in South Korea and Iraq each demonstrate similar personnel traits required for advisor selection. After action reviews and studies of KMAG and Iraq, recognize tactical and technical competence, command experience, cultural empathy, an interest in foreign culture, and patience as pre-requisites for advisor selection, yet the U.S. Army continues to ignore these characteristics when selecting and assigning personnel for advisory duty. In both KMAG and Iraq, the U.S. Army used no metric for filling advisory positions but assigned personnel for advisory duty based on availability for assignment and a need for combat experience. As seen in South Korea as well as Iraq, it is of the utmost importance to assign competent personnel with an interest and empathy towards foreign cultures.

In addition to advisor selection, advisors must receive cultural and language training to embed with counterparts. South Korean advisors received no specialized advisory training prior to assignment to KMAG, but after action reviews of KMAG acknowledge the requirement for cultural and language training prior to advisory duty. Ignoring KMAG studies, initial Iraq advisors, likewise, lacked advisory training, but the U.S. Army quickly realized the necessity of establishing a standardized advisory training model. Over time, the U.S. Army developed a sixty-day program of instruction that focused on combat skills and introductions to language and culture. As the advisory mission matured in Iraq, the U.S. Army established the 162nd Infantry Training Brigade to train advisors. One can hope that the 162nd Infantry Training Brigade represents initial U.S. Army efforts to institutionalize the advisory mission and continue to prepare soldiers

95

for future advisory missions. Security Force Assistance education and training must be instilled and interest in advisory fundamentals maintained throughout the conventional force so it may be applied successfully in future operations. Any future advisory mission must focus on cultural understanding to build rapport with host-nation counterparts. While language is fundamental to culture, the current advisory training apparatus cannot develop cultural and language experts.

Lastly, KMAG and Iraq advisory missions highlight the importance of sharing relevant tactics, techniques, and procedures amongst advisors. KMAG chiefly accomplished this through the KMAG Handbook, which acted as the medium to synchronize best practices across the R.O.K. Army. With the benefit of the communications age, Iraq advisors experienced near real-time access to relevant tactics, techniques, and procedures through professional publications, internet based knowledge sharing networks, blogs, and doctrine writing such as the counterinsurgency field manual. The U.S. Army must capture and institutionalize the hard fought lessons and experience developed from past advisory missions, and apply it to future Security Force Assistance missions.

What does this mean for future Security Force Assistance efforts? Current U.S. Army doctrine places the responsibility of advising and training host-nation security forces on the conventional modular Brigade Combat Team, and not the Special Forces.[8] —Thewo pillars of security force assistance are the modular brigade and Soldiers acting as advisors."[9] Current doctrine places the overall responsibility on the conventional force due to the size and scope of the mission.[10] However, not all soldiers in the conventional U.S. Army have the necessary skills to be successful advisors. Leadership in the U.S.

Army must prepare conventional forces to be military advisors, seek to understand why advisory techniques worked in the past, and work toward applying them in today's environment.[11]

What does the future hold for Security Force Assistance? While this thesis does not argue for a separate advisory corps, an argument made famous by Dr. John Nagl, it does drive home the point that the U.S. Army must not let the institutional knowledge about advisory missions gained from previous conflicts disappear.[12] Chief of Staff of the U.S. Army, General Casey, argued —this mission will not exist to the current scale in the near future; I'm just not convinced that anytime in the near future we're going to decide to build someone else's army from the ground up, and to me, the advisory corps is our Army Special Forces--that's what they do."[13] The current Vice Chief of Staff of the U.S. Army, General Chiarelli wrote a 2007 Military Review article expressing similar feelings as General Casey. He stated that Special Forces exist to advise foreign forces, and that the conventional force must be flexible enough to support this mission when the U.S. encounters a large advisory mission.[14] Notably, our doctrine identifies conventional brigade combat teams as the cornerstone of U.S. advisory missions, but the senior chain of command of the U.S. Army is still convinced that Special Forces take the lead when advising foreign forces. The debate continues on how to prepare for future advisory missions, but the story of KMAG provides valuable lessons for future Security Force Assistance efforts led by conventional U.S. Army personnel. U.S. Army leadership continues to see Security Force Assistance as a Special Forces mission, but conventional forces have advised foreign forces throughout history. If history is a predictor of the future, the conventional force must apply lessons from past advisory missions, and

educate the force to do it successfully in the future.

---

[1]Robert Sawyer, *Military Advisors in Korea: KMAG in Peace and War* (Washington, DC: Office of the Chief of Military History, 1962), 140.

[2]Robert Ramsey, *Advising Indigenous Forces: American Advisors in Korea, Vietnam, and El Salvador* (Fort Leavenworth, KS: Combat Studies Institute Press, 2006), 10.

[3]Callum A. MacDonald, *Korea, The War before Vietnam* (New York: The Free Press, 1987), 196-198.

[4]Max Hastings, *The Korean War* (New York: Touchstone), 324.

[5]Paik Sun Yup, *From Pusan to Panmunjom* (McLean: Brassey's, 1992), 241-242.

[6]Paul Braim, *The Will to Win* (Annapolis: Naval Institute Press, 2001), 272.

[7]Sun-Yup, *From Pusan to Panmunjom*, 244.

[8]U.S. Army, Field Manual 3-07.1, *Security Force Assistance* (Washington, DC: Government Printing Office, 2009), iv. U.S. Army Field Manual 3-07.1 states that the Combined Arms Doctrine Directorate, Combined Arms Center is responsible for sustaining interest in the advisory mission and maintaining Security Force Assistance. The Combined Arms Doctrine Directorate places Security Force Assistance responsibility on conventional U.S. Army forces.

[9]U.S. Army, Field Manual 3-07.1, *Security Force Assistance*, 2.

[10]U.S. Army, Field Manual 3-24, *Counterinsurgency* (Washington, DC: Government Printing Office, 2006), 6-3.

[11]David J. Kilcullen, *Counterinsurgency* (New York: Oxford University Press, 2010), 222.

[12]John Nagl, "Institutionalizing Adaptation: It's Time for a Permanent Advisor Command," *Military Review* (September-October 2008): 21.

[13]Yochi Dreazon, —U.S. Amy Still Struggles with How to School Iraqi Security Forces," *Wall Street Journal*, 29 February 2008, 4.

[14]Peter Chiarelli, Lieutenant General and Major Stephen Smith, —Learing From Our Modern Wars: The Imperatives of Preparing for a Dangerous Future," *Military Review* (September-October 2007): 8.

BIBLIOGRAPHY

Books

Appleman, Roy. *U.S. Army in the Korean War: South to the Naktong, North to the Yalu*. Washington, DC: Center of Military History, 1961.

Birtle, Andrew. *U.S. Army Counterinsurgency and Contingency Operations Doctrine 1860-1941*. Washington, DC: Center of Military History, 2003.

———. *U.S. Army Counterinsurgency and Contingency Operations Doctrine 1942-1976*. Washington, DC: Center of Military History, 2003.

Boal, Aaron. ─On the Ground: Training Indigenous Forces in Iraq." In *Turning Victory into Success*, edited by Brian De Toy. Fort Leavenworth, KS: Combat Studies Institute Press, 2004.

Bodansky, Yossef. *The Secret History of the Iraq War*. New York: HarperCollins Publishers, 2004.

Braim, Paul. *The Will to Win*. Annapolis: Naval Institute Press, 2001.

Brazinsky, Gregg. *Nation Building in South Korea*. Chapel Hill: University of North Carolina, 2007.

Chen, Jian. *China's Road to the Korean War*. New York: Columbia University Press, 1994.

Clark, Mark. *From the Danube to the Yalu*. New York: Harper's Publishers, 1954.

Cloud, David, and Greg Jaffe. *The Fourth Star*. New York: Crown Publishers, 2009.

Cordesman, Anthony, and Patrck Baet er. *Iraqi Security Forces: A Strategy for Success*. Westport, CT: Praeger Security International, 2006.

Cumings, Bruce. *The Origins of the Korean War*, 2 vols. Princeton: Princeton University Press, 1981, 1990.

Dorpalen, Andreas. *The Cambridge History of Warfare*. New York: Cambridge University Press, 1995.

Fontenot, Gregory, E. J. Degen, and David Tohn. *On Point*. Fort Leavenworth, KS: Combat Studies Institute Press, 2004.

Fuller, J. F. C. *The Foundations of the Science of War*. Fort Leavenworth, KS: U.S. Army Command and General Staff College Press, 1993.

Hastings, Max. *The Korean War*. New York: Touchstone, 1987.

Hermes, Walter. *U.S. Army in the Korean War: Truce Tent and Fighting Front*. Washington, DC: Center of Military History, 1966.

Kaufman, Burton. *The Korean War: Challenges in Crisis, Credibility, and Command*. New York: Alfred A. Knopf, 1986.

Kilcullen, David. *The Accidental Geurilla*. New York: Oxford University Press, 2009.

———. *Counterinsurgency*. New York: Oxford University Press, 2010.

Korea Institute of Military History. *The Korean War*. 3 vols. Lincoln: University of Nebraska Press, 2000-2001.

Lederer, William, and Eugene Burdick. *The Ugly American*. New York: W. W. Norton and Company, Inc., 1986.

Lowe, Peter. *The Origins of the Korean War*. London: Longman Group, 1986.

Macdonald, Callum. *Korea, The War Before Vietnam*. New York: The Free Press, 1987.

Millett, Allan. *The War for Korea, 1945-1950: A House Burning*. Lawrence: University Press of Kansas, 2005.

———. *The Korean War*. Washington, DC: Potomac Books, 2007.

Miscamble, Wilson. *From Roosevelt to Truman: Potsdam, Hiroshima and the Cold War*. Cambridge: Cambridge University Press, 2007.

Mortenson, Greg, and David Relin. *Three Cups of Tea*. New York: Penguin Group, 2006.

Nagl, John. *Learning to Eat Soup with a Knife*. Chicago: University of Chicago Press, 2005.

Ramsey, Robert. *Advising Indigenous Forces: American Advisors in Korea, Vietnam and El Salvador*. Fort Leavenworth, KS: Combat Studies Institute Press, 2006.

Sawyer, Robert. *Military Advisors in Korea: KMAG in War and Peace*. Washington, DC: Office of the Chief of Military History, 1962.

Selected Papers of the 2007 Conference of Army Historians. *The U.S. Army and Irregular Warfare 1775-2007*. Washington, DC: Center of Military History, 2008.

Sun-Yup, Paik. *From Pusan to Panmunjom*. Washington: Brassey's 1992.

Wright, Donald, and Timothy Reese. *On Point II*. Fort Leavenworth, KS: Combat Studies Institute Press, 2008.

Periodicals

Battaglia, Phillip, Colonel, and Lieutenant Colonel Curtis Taylor. —Securiy Force Assistance Operations: Defining the Advise and Assist Brigade." *Military Review* (July-August 2010): 2-9.

Chiarelli, Peter, Lieutenant General, and Major Stephen Smith. —Learing From Our Modern Wars: The Imperatives of Preparing for a Dangerous Future." *Military Review* (September-October 2007): 2-15.

Clemens, Peter. —Captain James Hausman, US Military Advisor to Korea, 1946-1948: —TheIntelligent Man on the Spot." *Journal of Strategic Studies* 25, no. 1 (March 2002): 163-198.

Huppert, Harry. —Korea Occupational Problems." *Military Review* 29 (December 1949): 9-16.

Kite, Jared, Captain, Major Christopher Matson, and Lieutenant Colonel Richard McConnell. —So You'reGoing to be on a MiTT." *Field Artillery* (November-December 2006): 39-42.

Millett, Allan. —Captai James H. Hausman and the Formation of the Korean Army, 1945-1950." *Armed Forces and Society* 23, no. 4: 503-539.

Nagl, John. —Istitutionalizing Adaptation." *Military Review* (September-October 2008): 21-26.

Sinclair, Duncan. —Operatins and Accomplishments." *Military Review* 27 (August 1947) 29-36.

Skaggs, David. —The Katusa Experient: The Integration of Korean Nationals into the U.S. Army, 1950-1955." *Military Affairs* 38, no. 2 (April 1974): 53-58.

Watson, Jeff. —Languageand Culture: Separate Paths." *Military Review* (March-April 2010): 93-97.

Government Documents

Department of the Army. Field Manual (FM) 3-07.1, *Security Force Assistance*. Washington, DC: Government Printing Office, May 2009.

———. Field Manual (FM) 3-24, *Counterinsurgency*. Washington, DC: Government Printing Office, December 2006.

———. Field Manual (FM) 7-0, *Training for Full Spectrum Operations*. Washington, DC: Government Printing Office, December 2008.

Eighth U.S. Army. *KMAG Handbook*. Eighth Army Publishing Directorate, 1951.

Foreign Relations of the United States of America. 1949 – Pt2: Far East and Australasia, United States Department of State. Washington, DC: Government Printing Office. http://images.library.wisc.edu/FRUS/EFacs/1949v07p2/M/0411.jpg (accessed 26 December 2010).

Froelich, Dean. *Military Advisors and Counterparts in Korea: A Case Study of Personal Traits and Characteristics*. Washington, DC: Research and Development Department of the Army, 1970.

Hausrath, Alfred H. *The KMAG Advisor: Role and Problems of the Military Advisor in Developing an Indigenous Army for Combat Operations in Korea*. Chevy Chase, MD: Operational Research Office, Johns Hopkins University, 1957.

Joint Center for International Security Force Assistance. *Commander's Handbook for Security Force Assistance*. Fort Leavenworth, KS: JCISFA, July 2008.

———. *Security Force Assistance Planner's Guide*. Washington, DC: Government Printing Office, 2009.

Joint Chiefs of Staff. Joint Publication 1-02, *Department of Defense Dictionary of Military and Related Terms*. Washington, DC: Government Printing Office, November 2010. http://www.dtic.mil/doctrine/new_pubs/jp1_02.pdf (accessed 18 March 2011).

Zbylut, Michelle, Kimberly Metcalf, Brandon McGowen, Michael Beemer, Christopher Vowels, and Jason Brunner. *Raw Comments from Cross-Cultural Survey attachment in An Analysis of Cross-Cultural Behaviors for Military Advisors in the Middle East*. Fort Leavenworth, KS: U.S. Army Research Institute for the Behavioral and Social Sciences and Joint Center for Security Force Assistance, 2008.

Other Sources

Chandrasekaran, Rajiv. —U.S. to Form New Iraqi Army." *The Washington Post,* 24 June 2003. www.iraqwararchive.org/data/jun24/US/wp06.pdf (accessed 14 March 2011).

Dreazon, Yochi. —U.S. Army Still Struggles with How to School Iraqi Security Forces." *Wall Street Journal,* 29 February 2008.

Engel, Richard, and Charlene Gubash. —Lasfull U.S. Combat Brigade Leaves Iraq." *MSNBC,* 19 August 2010. http://www.msnbc.msn.com/id/38744453/ns/ world_news-mideast/n_africa/ (accessed 14 March 2011).

Gibby, Bryan. ―Fighting in a Korean War: The American Advisory Missions from 1946-1953.‖ PhD diss., The Ohio State University, 2004.

Global Security. ―The Iraqi Army.‖ http://www.globalsecurity.org/military/world/iraq/nia.htm (accessed 14 March 2011).

Hudson, Curtis, Lieutenant Colonel, Commander 4th BN, 353rd Infantry Regiment, 162nd Infantry Training Brigade. Interview by author, 8 January 2011.

Iraq Coalition. ―Coalition Provision Authority Order # 2.‖ http://www.iraqcoalition.org/regulations/20030823_CPAORD_2_Dissolution_of_Entities_with_Annex_A.pdf (accessed 14 March 2011).

Jager, Sheila. ―Iraqi Security Forces and Lessons from Korea.‖ *Strategic Studies Institute Editorial* (December 2006).

Jamail, Dahr. ―No End in Sight as Fallujah Death Toll Approaches 700.‖ *The New Standard,* 11 April 2004. http://newstandardnews.net/content/index.cfm/items/169 (accessed 14 March 2011).

Lawrence, T. E. ―27 Articles.‖ *The Arab Bulletin, 1917.* http://wwi.lib.byu.edu/index.php/The_27_Articles_of_T.E._Lawrence (accessed 26 December 2010).

Lopez, Todd. ―Transition Team makes Officers Competitive for Promotion.‖ *Army.Mil News*, 3 July 2008. http://www.army.mil/-news/2008/07/03/10613-transition-team-experience-makes-officers-competitive-for-promotion/ (accessed 20 January 2011).

Nagl, John. *Institutionalizing Adaptation: It's time for a Permanent Army Advisor Corps.* Washington, DC: Center for a New American Security, 2007.

―Obama: U.S. to withdraw most Iraq troops by August 2010.‖ *CNN,* 29 February 2009. http://articles.cnn.com/2009-02-27/politics/obama.troops_1_iraq-troops-home president-obama?_s=PM:POLITICS (accessed 14 March 2011).

―President Bush Addresses the Nation.‖ *Washington Post,* 20 September 2001. http://www.washingtonpost.com/wpsrv/nation/specials/attacked/transcripts/bushaddress_092001.html (accessed 21 November 2010).

Wood, David, Lieutenant Colonel, Commander 1st BN, 353rd Infantry Regiment, 162nd Infantry Training Brigade. Interview by author, 8 January 2011.